SHADWELL'S RESTORATION COMEDY

Borgo Press Books by FRANK J. MORLOCK

Chuzzlewit
Congreve's Comedy of Manners
Crime and Punishment
Falstaff (with William Shakespeare, John Dennis, and William Kendrick)
Fathers and Sons
The Idiot
Jurgen
Justine
Lord Jim
Notes from the Underground
Oblomov
Outrageous Women: Lady Macbeth and Other French Plays (editor and translator)
Peter and Alexis
The Princess Casamassima
A Raw Youth
Shadwell's Restoration Comedy
The Stendhal Hamlet Scenarios and Other Shakespearean Shorts from the French (editor and translator)
The Widow's Husband; and, Porthos in Search of an Outfit: Two Dumasian Comedies (editor and translator)

SHADWELL'S RESTORATION COMEDY

A PLAY IN THREE ACTS

FRANK J. MORLOCK

THE BORGO PRESS
MMXII

Copyright © 1981, 2012 by Frank J. Morlock

FIRST BORGO PRESS EDITION

Published by Wildside Press LLC

www.wildsidebooks.com

For My Good Friend, Victor Lantang

CONTENTS

PREFACE. 9
CAST OF CHARACTERS. 11
ACT I, Scene 1 .13
ACT I, Scene 2 .49
ACT I, Scene 3 .63
ACT II, Scene 4. 81
ACT II, Scene 5. 99
ACT II, Scene 6. 145
ACT III, Scene 7 163
EPILOGUE. 229
ABOUT THE AUTHOR 231

PREFACE

It is said that a novelist writes the same novel over and over again. Whether this is true or not, it was certainly true of Thomas Shadwell, who wrote the same play over and over again, with more or less wit and different characters. Practically all the wit in this play is Shadwell's; the faults alone are mine. Shadwell was, in his own way, a very great writer. Unfortunately, while his wit is spread through his entire works, he is seldom revived. This is an attempt to give you Shadwell at his very best. The plot is based primarily on the plots to *The Woman Captain*, *The Squire of Alsatia*, *The Sullen Lovers*, and *The Virtuoso*.

CAST OF CHARACTERS

Sir Humphrey Blockhead-Swash, a dashing young rake
Lucy, his mistress
Valet/Steward to Sir Humphrey
Mrs. Letitia Scroop ("Captain Wildfire"), a former mistress of Sir Humphrey and wife to Scroop
Sir William Blockhead-Swash, Sir Humphrey's uncle, a censorious old man, father of Sir Christopher, much given to discipline
Mr. Gimrack Scroop, an elderly miser who fancies himself as a natural philosopher (a virtuoso), mistreats his young wife
Stanford, a young man of morose disposition much pestered with fools
Trim, a grand fop who believes himself as great an orator as he is magnificent in his taste in clothes
Prig, a crazy fop who is in love with all the women even though he has suffered for his folly
Sir Positive Atall, a man who knows everything about everything and will suffer no contradictions
Jack Tope, a genial old drunkard and a wit of the old school
Shamwell, a confidence man
Hackum (Captain Hackum), a swaggering coward
Sir Christopher Blockhead-Swash, a country bumpkin who rebels against his father and sets up for a gentleman
Bluffe (Sergeant Bluffe), a swaggering, cowardly gamester
Servant to Sir Christopher
Emilia, Lady Cheatly's daughter, a morose woman who does

not suffer fools gladly

Miranda, Lady Cheatly's younger daughter, a senseless flibbertigibbet in love with Mr. Trim

Lady Cheatly, a woman of a certain age much given to amorous intrigues and swindling

Striker, Mr. Trim's kept woman

Friske, Sir Christopher's kept woman

Lady Cheatly's Steward

Lady Cheatly's servant

Sergeant (the true Captain Wildfire), Mrs. Scroop's brother, a gigantic Army officer

Two soldiers

The scene is London, circa the Summer of 1676.

ACT I
SCENE 1

A luxuriously appointed bedroom, the residence of Sir Humphrey Blockhead-Swash. Sir Humphrey, a young rake of twenty-four, is dressed in a fashionable dressing gown. Lucy is in bed with no clothes on, crying. The time is about noon.

Sir Humphrey

Crying, my pretty miss?

Lucy

I hate you now.

Sir Humphrey

(approaching her and kissing her) I'll wager you lie. Did you not say you love me?

Lucy

Too much. I must never see you again.

Sir Humphrey

Can you be so hard-hearted?

(softly) I took you for a tender thing.

Lucy

Perhaps I may desire, now and then, a look— (cautiously) At a distance. But I will never venture near you again. (hugging the bedclothes to herself)

Sir Humphrey

If I thought you were in earnest, I should never let you go.

Lucy

I must go. I shall be missed. God, how will I ever look my mother in the face?

Sir Humphrey

Many a girl does the same as you did and manages to look like a saint. You must come to me every day.

Lucy

Never.

(A valet enters.)

Valet

Mrs. Scroop is coming up, sir.

Lucy

Oh! Hide me!

Sir Humphrey

Quickly! Into the closet.

(Lucy rushes into the closet, but some of her clothing is still lying on the bed. Exit valet. Enter Mrs. Scroop.)

Sir Humphrey

What wind blows you hither?

Mrs. Scroop

How dare you think that I, of all women, will suffer myself to be used in this way?

Sir Humphrey

You mean not used. That's your grievance.

Mrs. Scroop

You ingrate! Was I not yours and only yours?

Sir Humphrey

(coolly) Why, you were not married to me. I took no lease of your frail tenement. I was not a tenant at will.

Mrs. Scroop

Insolent! How dare you provoke my fury? Was ever woman's love like mine to thee? Perfidious man!

(weeping)

Sir Humphrey

After the thunder, the rain.

Mrs. Scroop

No. I scorn that you should bring tears to my eyes.

Sir Humphrey

Why do you come to trouble me, then?

Mrs. Scroop

Since I can please you no longer—I'll come to plague you. My ghost will come to haunt you.

Sir Humphrey

Indeed, your love was most peculiar with spitting and scratching. In your best humors, which were infrequent, you were always complaining and jealous to madness.

Mrs. Scroop

You devil incarnate.

Sir Humphrey

When you are old enough, your malice and ill humor will qualify you for a witch. You lack the softness to qualify for a mistress.

Mrs. Scroop

How dare you? For what dirty little wench am I treated like this? If she be above ground, I'll find her and tear her eyes out!

(looking around) Ha! By the bed, I see the slut has been here tonight. Oh, I cannot bear it.

(falling into a fit)

Sir Humphrey

(indifferently) You are a rare actress.

Mrs. Scroop

(leaping up) Is it so? Is it so? Devil, devil, I'll spoil your face for you. (she flies at him with claws bared)

Sir Humphrey

(retreating hastily) Will you force me to have my footman turn you out? (dodging)

Valet

(re-entering) Your uncle and Mr. Scroop are here, sir.

Sir Humphrey

'Sdeath. My uncle.

Mrs. Scroop

My husband.

Sir Humphrey

Madame, you may, if you wish, ruin both me and yourself. Try me once more and get into bed and cover yourself with the quilt. Hurry or I am undone.

Mrs. Scroop

(hesitating) Villain, you deserve to be ruined. But I love my honor too well.

Sir Humphrey

For heaven's sake, hide yourself in the bed, quickly.

Mrs. Scroop

I prefer the closet.

(Mrs. Scroop darts into the closet seconds before Sir. William Blockhead-Swash and his cousin Mr. Scroop enter.)

Sir Humphrey

Uncle, how unexpected. I beg your blessing.

Sir William

Heaven mend you; it can never bless you in the lewd course you are in.

Sir Humphrey

You are misinformed, sir. My course is not so lewd as you imagine.

Sir William

(to Mr. Scroop) Do you see? I am misinformed. He'll give me the lie!

(to Sir Humphrey) You were not drunk last night with bullies and roared and ranted, broke windows, raped and abducted a wench?

Sir Humphrey

No, I was not. I supped at home last night.

Sir William

And you are not called Squire Blockhead-Swash by your good-fo-nothing hangers-on, nor known as the Squire of Alsatia? Not you? No. No.

Scroop

(placatingly to Sir William) Perhaps it is a case of mistaken identity.

Sir William

You believe him! You make me mad, cousin Scroop. How many Blockheads are there in England, I ask you? Does he think to flim flam me with a lie?

Scroop

I am a great enemy to prodigality and wit, as you know. Still, your nephew has always been honorable in his business dealings with me, and has a reputation for being—err—reasonable in his pleasures.

Sir William

Only because my late brother, his father, was alive to check him in his wantonness.

Sir Humphrey

My father was ever indulgent to me, and I honor his memory.

Sir William

While you disgrace his name. Now that you are come into the estate, you are determined to waste it in a year. Remember, I am still trustee of half your estate.

Sir Humphrey

How could I forget, uncle?

Sir William

I will not allow you to marry any whore. You must have my permission to marry. Mark that. Mark that well.

Sir Humphrey

(bowing) I shall endeavor to secure your deserved approbation, uncle.

Sir William

(mollified) Well, well, that's well said. If I hadn't fought with one of your bullies this very morning—Captain Hackum—I should be wholly reconciled with you.

Sir Humphrey

Hackum? I know no one of that name.

Sir William

Well, well, nephew. Perhaps there was some mistake.

(A sudden roar from the closet.)

Lucy

(within) Murder, murder. Help, help!

(Mrs. Scroop, with her domino down over her face, pulls Lucy out by the hair.)

Sir Humphrey

Oh, damned she devil.

Mrs. Scroop

I'll make you an example, slut. Will you see him whether I will or not, you young whore!

Sir William

(excited to a fever pitch) Here's a nephew! Here's a nephew! Here's breeding! Here's a delicate nephew! Here's a dainty nephew! Thank God, my son is in the country and far away from your example.

Scroop

(hypocritically) I never thought this of you, Sir Humphrey.

Sir Humphrey

(hailing his valet) Out with this she bear. Out with her.

Mrs. Scroop

Revenge, you villain. Revenge.

(The valet enters with haste and carries her out struggling.)

Sir Humphrey

I can explain everything.

Sir William

This is the effect of whoring. Can't you content yourself with one harlot at a time?

Sir Humphrey

(defiantly) No, sir. It is the effect of not whoring. She rages because I have cast her off.

Scroop

She looked a little like my wife. Fortunately, I keep that would-be harlot safely locked up.

(The valet has returned. He is a little the worse for wear.)

Sir Humphrey

(to valet) See this innocent girl safe to her home. I charge you to protect her from that outrageous strumpet's fury.

Valet

It's more than I can answer for myself. May I take two footmen?

Sir Humphrey

Yes. Move briskly.

(Lucy and the valet go out.)

Sir William

(savagely, ironic) A sweet reformation. I am glad my brother is dead. It would break his heart.

Sir Humphrey

Sir, the young girl was never here before. She brought in the laundry. This furious wench, coming to rail at me, I put her in the closet. When you came, against my will, this one, too, ran into the closet.

Sir William

And her smock, nephew? Why did she forget her smock?

(he picks up the petticoat and brandishing it in Sir Humphrey's face) Did she come to wash her own clothes? Do you think you have your father to deal with? I leave you, nephew.

(Sir William rushes out in a fury. Scroop starts to follow Sir William.)

Sir Humphrey

A word with you, cousin Scroop.

Scroop

(pausing) I doubt I can help you with uncle William, cousin.

Sir Humphrey

Pshaw! He's all sound and fury. Never mind that. I shall need another two thousand pounds.

Scroop

I have a scruple against lending you money to spend it on whores. It is against my conscience.

Sir Humphrey

You may increase the interest.

Scroop

On the other hand, you have always been very punctual in paying your obligations.

(hesitates, weighing his scruples in one hand and his interest in the other) Very well. You shall have it. Twenty-five percent.

Sir Humphrey

Done.

Scroop

But I shall require a mortgage this time.

Sir Humphrey

You shall have it.

Scroop

I might have mentioned that my widowed sister, Lady Cheatly, has come to town, and is a very earnest business woman. You may wish to deal with her from time to time.

Sir Humphrey

I shall remember it. But I fear she is damnably ill-disposed towards me.

Scroop

That is true. But business is business. By the way, sir cousin, I am, as you know, a natural philosopher. I am planning to dissect a crustacean, vulgarly called a lobster. If you would care to witness this unusual event, you will have an opportunity to be present at one of the great scientific events of the last twenty years.

Sir Humphrey

I will attend, sir.

(low) I, too, am used to dissecting lobsters, but I usually eat them, too.

Scroop

Then, I shall expect you this afternoon.

(They bow to each other and Scroop exits.)

Sir Humphrey

Thank God, the old fool is too blind to recognize his own wife.

(hears a noise) Who waits there?

(Enter valet.)

Sir Humphrey

Prepare for a ball tonight. I shall want fiddlers, wine, and whores.

Valet

Do you take me for your pimp? I am your Steward.

Sir Humphrey

You provide me with all things necessary. Is anything as necessary as whores?

Valet

I served your father for twenty years and he never dared to ask me to do such a thing.

Sir Humphrey

Are you a man of means, good Mr. Morality? I'll get a Frenchman who will not quibble with his master.

Valet

You would not turn me away after all these years?

Sir Humphrey

Then trim your sails to the wind, sir. Pass me some perfume.

Valet

Perfume. Methinks it is unmanly.

Sir Humphrey

Consider what a stinking animal man is, exceeding all the beasts in stinking, and would you not have me mollify these natural imperfections?

Valet

I would have you clean and serving God.

Sir Humphrey

(impatiently) Pass the perfume.

(The valet obeys with obvious distaste. Sir Humphrey perfumes himself with great relish. Enter Stanford.)

Stanford

Not dressed, Sir Humphrey? You should be sharper for the game, considering the long fast you had at the hands of your father.

Sir Humphrey

One must savor one's pleasures, Stanford, and the women of this town, if you don't take care of your outside, will never let you be acquainted with their insides.

Stanford

You are mistaken. Men succeed now according to the clothes

they give, not the clothes they wear.

Sir Humphrey

Amongst your little whores, Stanford.

Stanford

Amongst your great whores, too, Sir Humphrey.

(changing the subject) At any rate, I am very glad to see you. I look on this as a place of refuge where I can escape my persecutors.

Sir Humphrey

Still complaining of fools, Stanford?

Stanford

Wherever I turn, I am baited.

Sir Humphrey

Why do you abuse this age so? Methinks it's as pretty a drinking and whoring age as a man could wish to live in.

Stanford

This morning, just as I was coming to you, Sir Positive Atall, that fool that will let no man understand anything in his company, virtually detained me by brute force.

Sir Humphrey

Sir Positive is very amusing.

Stanford

Another day like this and I shall enter a monastery.

Sir Humphrey

Pray heave it not be near a convent.

Stanford

My persecution did not end. After I granted his opinion, he forced me to stay an hour to hear his reasons for it But, no sooner had I, by some happy accident, (I shall still believe in miracles) got rid of the old pest, but in trots that insufferable puppy and world-renowned sportsman, Prig, who talked of nothing but racing and gambling.

Sir Humphrey

A very good companion for an hour.

Stanford

Then, having gotten rid of those two, who should appear, but that formal ass Trim, whose politeness would outdo a Chinese. At last I dodged him and came here.

Valet

(entering and announcing) Mr. Trim.

Stanford

I have but named the devil, and see, I have raised him. How the devil could he follow me? I took every precaution. I think the rascal has the nose of a bloodhound.

Sir Humphrey

Show the fool—err, gentleman—in. Now, we shall have a rare sport.

Stanford

Ye gods, is no place safe?

(Enter Trim)

Trim

Dear Stanford, and sweet Sir Humphrey, I am your most humble servant, and cannot but congratulate those auspicious stars that brought you hither to render your friends happy by your presence.

Sir Humphrey

(low) I have not stirred a foot these two years.

(to Trim) Your great civilities amaze me. I think there lives not among the race of mankind a person more skillful in all decencies of behavior, and all the arts of modish gallantry as to render him a wonder to all mankind as yourself.

(to Stanford) Disgusting fop.

Stanford

Now, have I reason or no?

Sir Humphrey

(to Trim, with a bow) Please be seated.

Trim

Not before you, sir. All England rings with your fame.

(Each strives to sit after the other.)

Trim

(lurching to his feet) Gad, but I like your breeches, Stanford. Your tailor shall make mine.

Stanford

His name is Wickham. You just have time to catch him before he closes.

Trim

But, it's just midday.

Stanford

He threatens to leave momentarily on an extended vacation.

Trim

But, I could not think of leaving you and Sir Humphrey so abruptly, even on such important business.

Stanford

Sir Humphrey won't mind; I'm sure I won't.

Sir Humphrey

I have heard you pay court to my widowed cousin Lady Cheatly.

Trim

(delighted to have an opportunity to deny it) I...I am her admirer, her adorer. I call her Dorinda and she honors me with the name Eugenius. I visit her daily.

Sir Humphrey

(teasingly) Nicknames and visits. There's something more between you than that?

Trim

Upon my honor, nothing.

Sir Humphrey

A likely story.

Trim

(rising, furious) I scorn your words.

Sir Humphrey

I did not think it was a dishonor for a man to lie with a pretty woman.

Trim

(proudly) I would not for the whole world. Nor did I ever.

Stanford

Why the devil do we all run after them and keep them company if not to lie with them?

Trim

(primly) I visit all the ladies for their conversation; for the excellence of their conversation.

Stanford

I'll tell you one thing, Mr. Trim, any woman you keep company with who does not think you have a mind to lie with her will never forgive you.

Trim

(genuinely shocked) You are obscene.

Sir Humphrey

I'll tell you one thing more. You must never be alone with a woman, but that you must offer, or she knows you care not for her. Five to one she grants. But if she does not care for you, she denies. Even so, she will like you the better.

Trim

Oh, uncharitable sentence! I, I who have succeeded in the affections of so many pretty creatures. If you did but see the advances that all the ladies make to me, you would stand amazed. I, I say, it is a chaste mind that wins all hearts.

Stanford

(disgusted) The devil, you say. Gentlemen, I have extraordinary business. I must leave you.

(Enter Prig.)

Prig

Gentlemen, good morrow. Where were you last night? But, never mind. I am come to get you to look at the best-bred horse in England. Woodcock was his grandfather. He is the son of Rednose, and cousin germane of Cock-a-Fart. I am going to make a civil visit to him. He's to run the race at Newmarket tomorrow.

Sir Humphrey

We cannot see him; we're engaged.

Stanford

Three days! A monastery!

Prig

Well then, let's make a match at tennis. I am invited to dine by two or three Lords, but if you will let me have pen, ink, and paper, I'll disengage myself.

Sir Humphrey

I tell you, I am engaged today.

Prig

We'll play or pay tomorrow at ten. Where shall we sup?

Stanford

Nowhere. You cannot sup.

Prig

Not sup?

Sir Humphrey

No. You are not fit to sup.

Prig

No? I am sure I have as good a stomach as any man in England. I will eat three meals a day with any man that wears a head.

Stanford

That will not do. (to Sir Humphrey) What am I condemned to?

Prig

No? I'll eat four then. What say you Stanford, will you play?

Stanford

Not for all the world.

Prig

A man must exercise or the ladies will not think him fit for exercise.

Stanford

Ladies are out of fashion.

Prig

How came women to be out of fashion?

Stanford

The women of this town are so unsound that it is safer to make war than make love. And our fops, who are cowards, prefer to admire themselves.

Sir Humphrey

I have a better way than exercise, I think.

Prig

Think? What a pox should a gentleman think of but dogs, horses, dice, tennis, races, and cockfighting. The devil take me, I never think of anything else, but now and then of a whore when I have a mind to her.

Sir Humphrey

Brave Prig, do you hold your humor still? Are you still in love with all women?

Prig

I venerate the sex. After dogs and horses.

Stanford

You have suffered more for them than all the knights errant in romances.

Prig

There is not a truer lover of all the sex than myself in all mankind. (twinges) What twinge was that?

(Trim shows signs of disgust as Prig talks.)

Sir Humphrey

So much love and so much pox never met together in one man since the creation. The druggists are very ungrateful fellows if they don't vote you a pension for the good you have done their trade.

Prig

Leave off fooling.

Trim

I would not wager six months for the term of your natural nose.

(Sir Humphrey claps Prig on the back.)

Prig

Oh! my shoulder—

Sir Humphrey

Better be a drunkard...wine breeds happiness, not diseases.

Prig

But beauty, heaven's brightest image, the thing which all the world desire and fights for, the spur of all glorious action—

Trim

(deeply affected) Sweet, poetic man. (embracing him) What sentiment.

Prig

Death! What have you done? You have murdered me. Oh, my neck and shoulders.

Trim

I humbly beg your pardon. I forgot this rheum is very strong.

Prig

Ah, is there a symptom I have not had? Ulcers, fistulas, pustules?

Sir Humphrey

How did you come by it?

Prig

Ah, the most delicate, civil young lady. A person of honor...a former mistress of the King.

Valet

(entering) A lady sends to you, Mr. Prig. She heard you were ill.

Prig

You see, Sir Humphrey, I am nobody with the ladies. Not I.

Trim

(jogging him) You dog.

Prig

(piteously) You hurt my arm.

Stanford

Gentlemen, detain me no further. I must go.

(starts to leave and jumps back) Good Lord, Sir Positive on the stairs. I had rather encounter an insurrection than meet him.

(Sir Positive enters.)

Sir Positive

Ah, dear Jack, have I found you?

Stanford

No, Sir Positive, you have not found me. I am just leaving.

Sir Positive

You shall not leave. I have just written a song.

Stanford

(desperately) I must take my leave of you. I must not lose my... business for a little music.

Sir Positive

Do you talk of music?

Stanford

I talk of my business.

Sir Positive

If any man in England gives you a better account of music than I do, I will give all mankind leave to spit on me. You must know it is a thing I have thought upon and considered and made my business since my cradle. Besides, I am so naturally a musician, that do re me were the first words I could speak. Do but ask Trim here.

Stanford

When shall I be delivered? Doubtless, I have sinned much.

Trim

Sir Positive has a great soul of music in him.

Sir Positive

Come, you shall hear it.

Sir Humphrey

(maliciously) Come, dear Sir Positive, make us happy.

Prig

Sir Positive will sing, and I shall dance.

Trim

He dances very finely.

Sir Positive

I defy any man in the world that outdoes him, for between you and me, I taught him every step he has.

Stanford

(desperate) Sir Positive, I am sorry I cannot. I must speak with a gentleman that leaves for France tonight.

Sir Positive

France! If any man gives you an account of France equal to mine, I'll suffer death! I have thought of their affairs...never speak more on it. 'Tis a lost nation. Absolutely undone. Take that from me. yet, were I in Paris with Cardinal Richelieu but one quarter of an hour, I'd put him in a way to save all yet.

Trim

I thought it was Cardinal Mazarin—

Stanford

Sir Positive, I am so much in haste that none but yourself should have stayed me of all mankind. (aside) Will I never escape?

Sir Positive

Mankind? Do you talk of mankind? I will give dogs leave to piss on me if any man understand mankind better than myself, now you talk of that. Between you and me, let me tell you, we are all mortal.

Stanford

I shall run mad.

Valet

(entering) Sir Positive, Lady Cheatly begs you would come look at her portrait that's come this morning. It's by Rembrandt.

(Exit valet.)

Sir Positive

There it is now, Stanford. She had as good as thrown her money in the dirt. If I had drawn the lines for him he might have made a good picture on it. Now you talk of painting.

(hesitating) Dear Stanford, I must go to her. Take it not unkindly.

Stanford

(as a man reprieved from execution) I will not. I will not.

Sir Positive

(genuinely troubled) A man must not disoblige his mistress.

(turns back)

Stanford

By all means not, Sir Positive. (aside) Great God in heaven, he's coming back.

Sir Positive

But, friendship, Jack. Friendship.

Stanford

(whispering to Sir Positive) If you do not go, Trim, who also aspires to her hand, will be before hand with you.

Sir Positive

Faith! You're right, Jack.

Stanford

Don't let me stop you. I swear I'll not take it ill.

Sir Positive

Let me hug you.

(Sir Positive briefly hugs Stanford and then rushes out.)

Trim

(in an indecent hurry) I, too, must leave suddenly, gentlemen. Your servant. Your servant.

(Trim rushes out.)

Stanford

That's a happy delivery.

Prig

Yes, that Trim is an unendurable fop.

Valet

(entering and announcing) Mr. Tope, sir.

(The valet exits and Tope enters.)

Sir Humphrey

Hail, hail, dear companion of the night.

Tope

My dear knight, my dear Sir Humphrey, you are the very prince of drunkards. Every night you clear the streets of bullies and idle rascals, sober citizens, and bilious cuckolds who should be home watching their wives.

Sir Humphrey

I am glad to find you so hearty.

Tope

Why, I roared with your grandfather. I have seen danger in my life! In those days a man could not go from the Rose Tavern to the Piazza once but he must venture his life twice.

Stanford

And the wine was better and the women handsomer. You old fellows are always magnifying the days of your youth.

Tope

Old! I have drunk off two generations, and I intend to drink off three more yet.

Sir Humphrey

Well, you buried my father.

Tope

Your father was a sober sot, a consumptive scoundrel. We could make nothing of him. He married like a puppy and grew most pitifully uxorious. But the comfort of it is that few of that sort get their own children. You are not a bit like him at all.

Stanford

Thank heaven, I never remember mine. Providence took care of me in good time.

Sir Humphrey

A health to my mistress. (offering wine)

Tope

I defy morning draughts. Trust an experienced drunkard, you will not live out half your days if you take this lewd course of drinking in the morning. I have buried two hundred morning drinkers of my acquaintance.

Sir Humphrey

I will have my mistress pledged. (offers wine again)

Tope

Your mistress! Which one? Every wench in a petticoat qualifies for that title, from humble trollop to bejeweled Duchess.

Prig

Tell us who it is.

Sir Humphrey

I am particular, damnable particular. I am fallen in love. I met her in church.

Stanford

See the danger of going to church. I warned you of it.

Tope

In love? Why, only till you get the wench; but when you have had her, you never fail to leave her, or a child by her, to the parish.

Sir Humphrey

Life in the work house is a good settled life. The sooner they take care of them, the better. But this is a lady of quality.

Tope

Stick with poor whores, my son, they are less troublesome and usually better-looking.

Sir Humphrey

A whore! This is a saint.

Prig

What a pox. I have never had as many whores as you, but I never had one whom I cared if she were hanged or no.

Tope

Seriously! A pox on your love. Love is a silly boyish disease and should never come after the chicken pox or mumps. A drunkard and in love! You will be as bad company as a pregnant chambermaid; worse, for she might be persuaded to take a cure. Love, ha, ha, ha.

Sir Humphrey

I am convinced every man will contract it before he dies. Look to it yet, Jack.

Tope

Why, this is a vile repenting strain, as if you were showing your parts at the gallows. Why don't you lay this lewdness on bad company and breaking the Sabbath?

Sir Humphrey

Old seducers, Jack. Old seducers.

Tope

No doubt you will soon want to be married!

Sir Humphrey

I do.

Prig

But, who is she?

Sir Humphrey

She's one of Lady Cheatly's daughters.

Prig

(stunned, aside) So! We are rivals.

Tope

I'm going. That a young man so promising should turn out just like his father. I thought your mother, at least, had better taste.

CURTAIN

ACT I
SCENE 2

A street in Alsatia.

Shamwell and Hackum meet Sir Christopher Blockhead-Swash and Bluffe.

Shamwell

Now you look like an heir indeed. You shine like a true gentleman.

Hackum

Give you joy, noble sir. Now you look like a true, gallant Squire.

Sir Christopher

I have been fortunate to light upon such true friends. I had never known breeding or gentility without you.

Shamwell

You buried all your parts in the country.

Sir Christopher

My father kept me in ignorance. I never saw such gentlemen as you in the country.

Bluffe

The world knows Mr. Shamwell and Captain Hackum are as complete gentlemen as ever came to Alsatia.

Sir Christopher

Well, I protest. I am so fine, I don't know where to look upon myself first. I don't think the Lord Mayor's son is finer.

Shamwell

He is a scoundrel compared to you.

Sir Christopher

Let me embrace you all.

(they hug each other) Devil take me, but we are mad fellows.

(roaring) God, we had a rare night of it; kicked the watch; kissed whores; stormed bawdy houses, and committed sundry other outrages to the confusion of the citizenry. Ha, ha, ha.

Bluffe

On my soul, we broke a hundred pounds worth of windows.

Sir Christopher

Am I not a gay spark?

Hackum

We kept Covent Garden working last night, I'll vow.

Bluffe

We overran the town as Alexander overran Asia.

Sir Christopher

Lord, what will Sir William say when he learns I am in London?

Shamwell

What matter what he says? Is not every foot of the estate entailed upon you?

Sir Christopher

To hell with him! I can endure it no longer. I'll teach him to use his son like a dog. Let us go to see my cousin, Sir Humphrey.

Shamwell

You shall not see him till you outshine him every way. Your cousin's heart shall break in envy of your gallantry. All the whores will ogle you and fall before your feet like the ancients worshipping Priapus!

Sir Christopher

Tell me once more what we did last night. Some action I remember, but the better part is all darkness to me. Yet it runs in my head that we had a fray.

Bluffe

We did indeed.

Sir Christopher

But, what execution was there? Whose skull cracked? Whose lungs pierced?

Hackum

Why, it was a mere nothing. You had a skirmish with some drunken rascal and Brigadier Stokes with a detachment of the watch who fell in and routed both parties. Two of the watch had slight hurts which they are ready to swear are mortal, and two of your footmen were carried to the roundhouse.

Sir Christopher

An evening very handsomely spent. But, see my footmen ransomed. But, what else?

Bluffe

This magnificent hero, this thunderbolt of war, this Captain Hackum, laid about him like Tamerlane or else the watch had mauled us.

Sir Christopher

It seems to me there was a woman.

Shamwell

You took a gentleman's wench away by force.

Sir Christopher

(beaming) Did I so? But, does her gallant roar for her?

Hackum

He dares not, the scoundrel. He knows me.

Shamwell

It would take a volume to write the history of your conquests.

Sir Christopher

But, where is the wench?

Shamwell

Well, sir, it must be admitted she was not very handsome, nor over well dressed, nor extremely clean...and though you put her to bed in your own bed, when you returned after having recovered a little and went to your bed...you puked at the sight of her and threw her, naked, out of the house.

Sir Christopher

It was very impudent of the ugly strumpet to come hither.

Hackum

The nation will ring of us. Such exploits, such achievements. Not a window in all the inns of Chancery; those hives of attorneys, those suit breeders, those litigious rogues—

Bluffe

Then, how we scoured the market people, overthrew the butter women, defeated the pippin merchants, wiped out the milk men, pulled off the door knockers, repainted the gilt signs—

Hackum

We have scoured these three nights so magnificently that we were taken for your cousin, Sir Humphrey Blockhead–Swash and his company.

Sir Christopher

Sir Humphrey? No, no. Sir Humphrey is the finest, a most complete gentleman that ever wore a head.

Hackum

There are others, Squire, that shall be nameless.

Sir Christopher

Oh, no. Never talk on it. There will never be his fellow. Had you seen him, as I did, when he cleared the Rose Tavern. In a minute's time he had cleared the whole house and broke all the windows. Well, well, he shall be my pattern while I live. Oh, if you did but hear him curse and swear, you'd be in love with him; like music from an organ.

Hackum

Pretty gentleman, I confess; but time shall try. I'll say no more.

Sir Christopher

All Europe cannot show a braver gentleman. Oh, if fate and my own industry could ever make me like this dear, this gallant, Sir Humphrey, I were at the end of my ambition. The finest man that ever beat a constable.

Servant (entering)

Sir, some of the inhabitants of one of the houses whose windows you broke last night have learned your name. They have gotten the Lord Chief Justice to issue a warrant against you.

Sir Christopher

Is this true?

Servant

By the mass, it is.

Shamwell

No matter. We'll bring you off. Trust me for that.

Sir Christopher

Dear friend, I rely on you for everything.

Bluffe

In this part of London, we value not their writs and summons.

Shamwell

The King's writ does not run in Alsatia. There has not been a writ served here these ten years.

Hackum

If any of the King's officers dare invade our privileges, we'll send them to hell without bail or main prize.

Servant

I have also learned that your father is in town searching for you.

Sir Christopher

Sir William! Impossible.

Shamwell

Courage, my heir entail. Your father's a poor sneaking tenant for life. You shall ignore him. And if we do put a debt upon the estate, I have designed an heiress for you who shall take it all off.

Hackum

If you meet your father, stick up thy countenance or thou art ruined, my son of promise. When he approaches, we'll all pull down our hats and cry, bow wow.

Sir Christopher

Bow wow. I'll do it.

(Enter Sir William, not seeing Sir Christopher at first.)

Sir Christopher

My father! Hide me, let's sneak out.

Hackum

It's the same old fellow I had like to have had a fight with this morning.

(aside) Who would have thought the mean-tempered wretch would have dared to fight?

Shamwell

Let me talk to him a little.

Sir William

Is he fallen into these hands? His estate is spent before he has it.

(to Hackum) Oh, bully rascal, there you are.

Hackum

I could whip thee through the lungs easily, but I'll desist at present.

(aside) Old piss and vinegar!

Sir William

I would speak with Sir Blockhead-Swash.

Shamwell

Why, look you, sir, according to your assertion of things,

doubtful in themselves, you must be forced to grant that whatsoever may be, may also well not be, in their own essential differences and degrees. Therefore—

Sir William

(with icy menace) Where is my son?

Shamwell

Your question consists of two terms, the one "ube" where: but of that I say nothing because there is no son or anything belonging to you to be the subject matter of debate. Forasmuch as your son being somewhat obliquely, which you, out of a mature gravity, may have weighed and think too heavy to be undertaken; what does it avail you if you shall precipitate or plunge into affairs as unsuitable to your physiognomy as they are to your complexion?

Sir William

Do you hear me, sir? Let me see my son. Offer to banter me once more and I will cut your throat.

Sir Christopher

(peeping out from behind Bluffe and Hackum) Do you love your life? The Captain is a lion.

Sir William

An ass, is he not?

Hackum

If you were not the father of my dearest friend, I don't know what my honor would prompt me to do.

Shamwell

My honor will not let me strike your father.

Bluffe

Nothing can provoke me against the father of my noble friend.

Shamwell

We have respect for your blood.

Sir Christopher

You see how their friendship prevails over their valor?

Sir William

Valor. Here's valor. (kicking them.)

Shamwell

Nothing shall make me transgress the rules of honor.

Sir William

Will not this convince you of their cowardice?

Sir Christopher

I am sure they are valiant. Have they not overthrown the watch many times?

Sir William

(kicking them again) Let us try again.

Hackum

Damn me, Squire, I don't like this.

Shamwell

God, he kicks with iron toes.

Sir William

What, do you take me to be in jest?

Bluffe

Aye, why are you not?

Sir William

I shall put you out of doubt of that presently.

Hackum

What the devil do you mean?

Bluffe

Do not provoke me further.

Shamwell

If you be uncivil 'tis time to take a course with you. Help, help! An arrest, an arrest.

Hackum

An arrest, a bailiff.

Sir William

You dogs! Am I a bailiff?

Shamwell

You will be used as one, you old wasp. An arrest!

(The mob enters through the windows, prepared to defend its territory with pots, pans, muskets, swords, pikes, and every conceivable type of improvised weapon. It could be a scene from the French Revolution.)

Sir William

I must run or I'll be pulled to pieces. Impudent dogs. An arrest, an arrest. My heels must save my life.

(All run off in several directions as the scene ends.)

ACT I
SCENE 3

St. James Park.

Emilia and Miranda enter.

Emilia

Do not pester me about men, Miranda. I can't stand them. They are all such fools.

Miranda

Mr. Trim is the finest person, so well-bred. It would do one good to have such a bedfellow.

Emilia

He's a fool. He has no wit and all he does is talk.

Miranda

I don't care for a wit. But I can listen to Mr. Trim all day long. He tells such pretty stories of himself.

Emilia

I should rather a man talked about me than himself. Good Lord, he's coming.

Trim

(entering) Good ladies, I am your vassal couchant.

Emilia

Let me escape.

Trim

I have a little dog for you, Miss Miranda, which I intend to present as a hieroglyphic of my affection.

Emilia

(aside) I shall enter a nunnery. (aloud) I must leave you, I have the most pressing business.

Trim

Do not leave, Miss Emilia, I adore your shoestrings.

Emilia

My business will not wait.

(Emilia runs off in haste.)

Trim

Dear me. She left.

Miranda

Surely you don't mind being alone with me, Mr. Trim?

Trim

(gallantly) It was my fondest wish.

(Enter Sir Humphrey, who observes Trim and Miranda.)

Sir Humphrey

Now, why must I love a fool who loves another fool?

(approaching Miranda and Trim) Madame, your humble servant. Mr. Trim, yours also.

Trim

Sir Humphrey, how pleasant to see you again so soon. Have you been to Court today?

Sir Humphrey

No, sir.

Trim

I am sure I was missed and it was remarked upon. But I mind nothing when such a pretty creature as Miss Miranda is in the way.

Miranda

(delighted) You are pleased to say so, sir.

Sir Humphrey

(whispering) I mean to be revenged upon you for making me fall in love with you.

Miranda

(naive, but excited) Why, what will you do to me?

Sir Humphrey

I'll have no mercy upon you.

Miranda

(interested) Really? How?

Trim

(vacantly) I shall have a new suit tomorrow.

Miranda

Isn't Mr. Trim the most modish genteel person?

Sir Humphrey

(aside, disgusted) What an entertainment is this to me, that I should love such a thing?

(to Miranda) Do not mistake him, he's a perfect ass, I assure you.

Miranda

What a thing to say. He does everything so like a gentleman.

(Trim takes some snuff very modishly.)

Sir Humphrey

Like a gentleman? He's a clown; he has not breeding enough to be a valet.

Miranda

You wits never speak well of each other.

Sir Humphrey

Why do I love such a brainless idiot?

Trim

What color do you fancy my suit, dear Miss Miranda? I think purple would go best with my complexion.

Miranda

Oh yes, purple would be very modish.

Trim

(proudly) My fancy always pleases the ladies.

Sir Humphrey

Do you know that I will not suffer you to smile, cringe, and play the monkey here?

Trim

(serenely) I cannot help it; if ladies will love me and be affected by my person, what is it to me?

Sir Humphrey

(shoving Trim) I'll endure this no longer. Begone.

Miranda

(angrily) What have you done to poor Mr. Trim?

Trim

(pettishly) I wonder you should have no more breeding; one would have thought you had learned more from me by this time.

Miranda

(fussing over him) Let me help you. I'll set you right again.

Sir Humphrey

What's this!

Trim

Devil take me if I could not find it in my heart to ruffle your cravat before the lady for this outrage of yours.

Sir Humphrey

Leave us, sir, or I'll cut your throat.

Trim

Well! I cannot be ill-bred, though you can. Therefore, I shall take my leave.

(Trim exits with all the dignity of an offended Peacock.)

Miranda

(upset) What have you done? You have made Mr. Trim go away. I'll follow him.

Sir Humphrey

(aside, in a fury) She can't leave me for that fop.

(Miranda has followed Trim and Sir Humphrey follows Miranda. Enter Emilia and then Stanford. They walk up and down, taking little notice of each other.)

Emilia

I am the greatest object of pity that was ever seen. I am never free from importunate fools, my sister is a flibbertigibbet and my mother tries to keep me under lock and key, and will marry me to the first wealthy fool that comes along.

Stanford

I am no less afflicted with fools than that young lady.

Emilia

There is no possibility of relief but to leave the world.

Stanford

Who would live in an age when fools are reverenced and impudence esteemed?

Emilia

In so corrupt an age, when almost all mankind flatter the rich and oppress the poor.

Stanford

(listening) This is pleasant. As if she were not as bad as anyone.

Emilia

Now this fellow has a design to have me think him wise.

Stanford

Now the illiterate fool despises learning.

Emilia

Among the learned we find many that are great scholars by art and are fools by nature.

Stanford

This shall not persuade me that she is not one herself.

Emilia

Now he thinks to be taken for a discreet fellow, but this will not do. Well, I will leave this world immediately.

Stanford

Which way do you intend to go?

Emilia

Why do you ask?

Stanford

That I may be sure to take another way.

Emilia

Nothing could so soon persuade me to tell you as that.

Stanford

May in inquire your name, madame?

Emilia

Why would you want to know it?

Stanford

That I may avoid you.

Emilia

In order to gratify so fond a wish, know that I am Emilia Cheatly.

Stanford

Lady Cheatly's daughter?

Emilia

None other.

Stanford

I had heard that lady had two daughters. One sensible, the other a dizzy creature.

Emilia

Very true.

Stanford

I fear you must be the troublesome one.

Emilia

Impertinent. It is my sister. She dotes on men, especially fops. I am sure she would find you charming.

Stanford

Most women dote on fops. Surely you do not pretend to be an exception?

Emilia

And most men love a flibbertigibbet.

Stanford

When did you see a man so foolish as a woman?

Emilia

When I see you.

Stanford

No, no. No man will ever rival a woman in folly.

Emilia

That's hard. I find nothing but owls among the best of you.

Stanford

This is not altogether so much impertinence as I expected from a woman. But, let me tell you, I have too often suffered by women not to fear the best of them.

Emilia

I must confess you are not so ridiculous as the rest of mankind. I would give money to see a man that is not so.

Stanford

This looks like sense. I find she does understand something. A miracle for a woman.

Emilia

This is not so foppish as I believed, yet it is very impertinent of you to tell me what I know already.

Stanford

I am sure not many of your sex have such discernment.

Emilia

I am sure you have little. You cannot distinguish between those that have and those that have not.

Stanford

I find I can endure you better than most women.

Emilia

To be honest with you, you are not so troublesome a fop as I expected.

Stanford

(aside) What the devil makes me think this woman attractive?

(to Emilia) I can bear this with patience, but if you should grow troublesome, I shall run away presently.

(aside) What an owl I am to like her.

Emilia

Pray heaven you don't give me the first occasion to flee. (aside) Well, I don't know what's the matter, but I like this man strangely. What a fool I am.

Stanford

(aside) I don't care how long I am with her.

Emilia

I see my mother coming. If she sees me, she will lock me up or pester me to receive Mr. Trim or Sir Positive Atall. I must hide.

Stanford

Let me assist you.

(Emilia and Stanford hurry out together. Enter Lady Cheatly, with a fan. Tope enters after her, in hot pursuit.)

Lady Cheatly

Are there no gallants left? Poor gentle love is now neglected, and all men's heads lie towards knavery and business, like my brother, Scroop. I have walked the whole length of the Mall alone on purpose for an amorous adventure and met none; (vexed) none except this old, red-nosed, battered drunkard.

Tope

She is richly laden. I'll board her. Sure she is an alderman's wife. I have not cuckolded an alderman these seven years. Pray she be sound— She's of quality, but may be no sounder for that. Hail, solitary damsel. By thy pensive walking, I find thou art in distress, and being a true knight errant, come to offer thee the succor of my person.

Lady Cheatly.

Not in so much distress as to require help from you.

Tope

Come, I know what you want.

Lady Cheatly

What, do you think I have a mind to drink a bottle or two?

Tope

You take my meaning well enough.

(leering) Have at you!

Lady Cheatly

Hold, hold. Methinks you are an ancient gentleman.

Tope

Ancient! God take me, I am tough and well-seasoned. All this younger generation are starvelings and have the rickets.

Lady Cheatly

Do not grow troublesome.

(aside) Why is it my luck to catch an old pig when I want a young stud.

Tope

Troublesome? Don't be foolish. Don't push the dainty aside until you have tasted it.

Lady Cheatly

Taste your dainty? I'm sure it's stale.

Tope

Stale! You don't know what's in me.

Lady Cheatly

Last night's lewd dose and two bottles this morning. That an old gentleman with one foot in the grave should be thus lewd.

Tope

(aside) I'll kick her. But, I'll dissemble. A whore she is, my whore I'll make her. (aloud) Come dear, do not take me for a milk sop. Women are born to be controlled.

Lady Cheatly

Old gentleman, be civil.

Tope

Old again! You're going to get it now. I know what you are come for and you shall not go without it. Come, come, wench.

Lady Cheatly

You are a saucy fool and I'll have you kicked.

Tope

(grabbing her) Come, come, you shall go.

Lady Cheatly

Help, help!

(Enter Stanford)

Stanford

How now, Jack, ravishing?

Lady Cheatly

A thousand thanks for delivering me from the assaults of this libidinous old goat.

Stanford

So fine a lady shall never want any service I can do her.

Lady Cheatly

Any service, sir? Sweet sir, your manner is as obliging as your person.

Stanford

Do not worry about Jack. Say what he will, he is as harmless a man to a lady as can be.

Lady Cheatly

I knew it instantly.

Tope

Now I see her face, take her and make your best on it.

Lady Cheatly

Shall I, who, in my not too distant youth, charmed all gallants even to fascination and have been adored by the Lords Spiritual and Temporal, be thus slandered? Know, I have more beauty than you can make use of, poor railing buffoon.

Tope

Whoever commits adultery with thee, it must be merely the act of the devil; there's nothing o the flesh in it. You out paint the Whore of Babylon.

Lady Cheatly

'Tis false, rude fellow. I only use a wash. A mere wash.

Tope

No more does a wall. You would appear by art a beauty, but are by nature, a mummy.

Lady Cheatly

Was there ever so rude a person?

Tope

Why thou piece of clockwork, thou hast no teeth, no hair, no eyebrows nor complexion but what cost thee money. There's wit, old sybil.

Stanford

You know where you are, sir?

Tope

(not flinching) What, sir?

Stanford

(aside to Tope) Jack, dissemble. There's a trick in it.

Tope

Pox on her. I care not if she were hanged.

(Exit Tope.)

Lady Cheatly

Please protect me to my house. There I shall try to make some measure of return for this favor. I assure you there is not a person living who has more ways of showing gratitude than I.

Stanford

I am your slave, madame.

Lady Cheatly

I have something to impart to you in which I would not willingly meet an interruption. Let us retire to a more fitting place.

(Stanford and Lady Cheatly exit arm in arm.)

CURTAIN

ACT II
SCENE 4

A room in Sir Humphrey's house, later the same evening.

Sir Humphrey

I wonder what keeps Stanford?

(Tope looks as if he would explain, then changes his mind.)

Sir Humphrey

No matter. We shall feast with the best of foods, the rarest of wines, the choicest music, the best of women.

Tope

Whores, you mean?

Sir Humphrey

What use can we make of honest women?

Tope

None.

Sir Humphrey

Whores, I do mean: with whom after we have danced and dined—we'll take to scented baths and there—soak—till we be refreshed.

(Enter Striker, Friske, and Lucy.)

Sir Humphrey

Here's my mistress.

Striker

We come to wish you joy.

Sir Humphrey

You bring it with you.

Tope

Are these whores?

Sir Humphrey

Whores? That's a dirty word. There are no whores but poor whores. These are ladies.

Striker

You are the pattern of all knights. You keep your mistress so fine.

Sir Humphrey

I yield to Mr. Trim. He starves his mother to keep you in style.

Striker

I must confess he does pretty well.

Sir Humphrey

Why didn't you bring him?

Striker

If I did, he'd always be going about with me. I am too much a lady to permit that!

Friske

I wish I could control Sir Christopher the way you govern poor Trim. I should be a princess.

Lucy

(softly) I don't want to govern you, my dear. I want nothing but your love.

Sir Humphrey

(to a footman) Send for music! I'll please all my senses at once. I hate a man who is a mere drunkard or a mere wencher.

Tope

There spake an oracle.

Footman

Mr. Scroop.

(Enter Scroop.)

Scroop

Good evening, Sir Humphrey. I have brought the mortgage.

Sir Humphrey

Sit down and eat with us, cousin.

Scroop

I will not eat meat.

Tope

Have a little beer or wine.

Lucy

Let us not mind this brute.

Striker

Filthy fellow! Will he not please his stomach?

Sir Humphrey

Here are fine ladies! Here's a sight for you.

Scroop

I am married. This is abominable, profane, scandalous.

Lucy

I hear he keeps his wife locked up.

Striker

I have heard that; but I also have heard she has a way to get out.

Sir Humphrey

You scandalize the ladies. I will sign and seal. Let us withdraw.

(Exit Sir Humphrey, Lucy, and Scroop.)

Tope

Sweet Mrs. Striker, shall we make use of this opportunity?

Striker

I would not be false to Mr. Trim for all the world.

Tope

But he's ugly and foolish.

Striker

But he's good-natured and keeps me in high style.

Prig

(who has been talking with Friske) True to Sir Christopher? Surely, you'll not be so unfashionable a thing as to be faithful?

Friske

I have a conscience, sir.

Prig

True, he pays for your body; but it is not fit he should have your soul.

Striker

(interrupting and laughing) That will not serve your turn.

Prig

Give me the soul and I shall soon have the body.

Friske

Not mine, sir. Shall it ever be said that I am false to Sir Christopher?

Prig

Should it ever be told, he'd not believe it.

Friske

I desire but to visit you while Sir Christopher is unfit because of drink.

Prig

Why, that is every day. Kind thought.

(Enter Sir Christopher with Hackum and Bluffe. Sir Christopher is singing.)

Friske

It's my gallant and his rough friends. (she moves to Tope)

Hackum

Who's that talking with your wench?

Bluffe

Shall I pluck out porker and run him through?

Sir Christopher

No, no, he's an honest fellow: Jack Tope. As mad as the rest of us. How now, Jack Tope? We have had a rare night of it.

Tope

Greetings, dear, hopeful boy.

Friske

(to Sir Christopher) Oh, my dear. Why did you expose yourself to such danger, knowing how fondly I love you?

Sir Christopher

Peace, no harm done; we only broke a hundred pounds worth

of windows. Please know my friends Captain Hackum and Sergeant Bluffe.

(Hackum and Bluffe make up to Striker as quickly as they can, after exchanging bows with the rest of the company. Re-enter Sir Humphrey and Lucy.)

Sir Humphrey

Cousin Scroop has made me promise to come to see him dissect a lobster later this evening.

Lucy

Surely you won't go?

Sir Humphrey

I may. Cousin Christopher, your servant.

Sir Christopher

May I present Captain Hackum and Sergeant Bluffe?

Sir Humphrey

Great names, indeed, but they are somewhat negligent in their toilet.

Sir Christopher

Never mind that; they are as brave as lightning.

Lucy

They look rather dreadful. Come, ladies, there are cards within.

(The three women go out.)

Sir Christopher

Each of them has killed his man. But they are good fellows and sing the purest bawdy songs. Hey, are we not mad fellows?

(Re-enter Trim.)

Trim

Sir Humphrey, your humble servant.

Sir Humphrey

Sweet, Mr. Trim.

Trim

Where is Mrs. Striker?

Sir Humphrey

Within with Lucy and Mrs. Friske.

Trim

I long to see the pretty rogue. I have not seen her these two hours.

(seeing Sir Christopher) Oh, God, Sir Christopher and his bullies. Hide me! They threaten to fight with me if I will not drink and play at dice.

Sir Christopher

(spying Trim) Where is the scoundrel that will not drink! Draw, sir, I will tap you and let out the wine you have already drunk.

Sir Humphrey

Good cousin, spare his life for my sake.

Sir Christopher

For your sake, he lives, but on the condition he shall drink and play.

Trim

Commit not a rape on me. I never drink between meals. I would not be intoxicated for the universe.

Sir Humphrey

(examining Sir Christopher) Have you been in a fight?

Sir Christopher

A skirmish, a mere skirmish.

(Trim has been playing dice with Hackum and Bluffe.)

Trim

Gentlemen, let me give over play. You have gotten my gold watch and diamond ring and twenty pounds to boot.

Bluffe

You shall play another twenty pounds, by God.

Trim

What would you have of a man? I can't abide gambling.

Hackum

You don't take us for cheats, do you?

Trim

Not for the world.

Hackum

(menacingly) You'd best not.

Bluffe

Will you play or no?

Trim

Double or quits.

(They roll the dice.)

Trim

Double ten. I'm quit.

Bluffe

It was a seven.

Hackum

(to Bluffe) If you do this, you'll lose him forever.

Bluffe

Was it double ten?

Hackum

He's in the right.

Bluffe

It's your trick, but you shall not go.

(Enter Lucy, Striker and Friske.)

Striker

Is he here? Now you shall see how to treat a man.

Trim

My dear, are you here?

Striker

Yes, you fop. But, why are you here?

Trim

Don't be angry. I came to escort you home.

Striker

I'll not go. Go home by yourself. Go, I say. Go quickly.

Trim

Dear Striker, let me stay.

Bluffe and Hackum

Ay, let him stay.

Striker

Shall I have people think you are jealous of me? How dare you to come after me?

Trim

Jealous! I scorn their words.

Striker

Go home, then! Why do you stay when I bid you go? Do you think you are fit to be seen in good company because I am?

Lucy

Let me intercede for him.

Striker

He shall not stay. If I should suffer him to stay, he'd always be peeking after me.

Trim

I'll give you all the money I have about me if you'll let me stay.

Striker

Let me have it.

Trim

There.

Striker

Well, I'll go home with you. Wait outside for me for an hour until I am ready.

(Enter Scroop, ready to leave.)

Scroop

Good evening, cousin. I must go home to take a swimming lesson. At nine precisely, I will dissect the crustacean.

Sir Humphrey

I will be there, cousin.

Scroop

Mr. Trim, you here? You promised to be present at my swimming lesson. Will you come?

Trim

Why, so I did. Dear Striker, may I go?

Striker

Very well, go. But, don't flirt.

(Scroop and Trim bow themselves out.)

Sir Humphrey

Sir Christopher, Jack Tope, a word with you. This foolish cousin of mine has made me promise to watch him dissect a lobster. Gentlemen, a design comes into my head of carrying this company, women and fiddlers, to that wretch's house.

Sir Christopher

Did I not tell you, Hackum, there was not a finer knight in Christendom?

Lucy

We shall certainly have very good sport.

Tope

That's well. 'Twill frighten him out of his wits, and perhaps, free his wife in the bargain.

Sir Humphrey

I have a design against his niece Lady Cheatly's daughter.

Tope

Does that witch lodge with him?

Sir Humphrey

Yes. And I love one of her daughters.

Tope

Which one?

Sir Humphrey

I don't know.

Tope

Perhaps I shall be revenged on this Lady Cheatly. For that was she I met in the Mall today.

Sir Humphrey

And Mrs. Scroop, who was once my mistress and has caused me great embarrassment today, will be obliged to meet me and keep her tongue quiet.

Sir Christopher

'Tis resolved, then. We'll tear the ground, roar, and make more noise than a sea fight.

Sir Humphrey

Well said, Sir Christopher. Do you hear? (to a footman) Bid all my coaches come to the gate. Prepare baskets of wine and food.

Sir Christopher

But, we must first let him get home. There's time for a bottle or two. Come, let's march, brave Bluffe and Hackum. To the wars!

(Exeunt singing.)

CURTAIN

ACT II
SCENE 5

The home of Scroop and his sister Lady Cheatly.

Lady Cheatly and Stanford enter, arm in arm.

Lady Cheatly

And that's the bedroom.

Stanford

Delightful house.

Lady Cheatly

I swear you are the most gallant and proficient gentleman in this town.

Stanford

You flatter me, madame.

Lady Cheatly

It's a shame you keep company with such a scoundrel as Sir Humphrey.

Stanford

He's your cousin, is he not?

Lady Cheatly

Yes, but he's a rake. I am afraid to allow him near my house for fear he'll debauch my daughters.

Stanford

But, madame, he's a man of sense. There are so few in this town. I am persecuted with fools.

Lady Cheatly

That's true. But a woman of fashion and business such as myself must put up with fools, dear Stanford. Otherwise we should lack the opportunity to meet men of sense such as yourself.

Stanford

You are too kind, Lady Cheatly.

Lady Cheatly

You may call me Honora.

Stanford

Honora. Will you introduce me to your family?

Lady Cheatly

I hesitate to introduce you to my daughters. They are such forward young sluts and have no manners. The women of today are not brought up to be ladies.

Stanford

I am sure that your daughters cannot fail to be like their mother. (aside) I am in love with her daughter.

Lady Cheatly

Have you heard of the fame of my brother, Sir Gimrack Scroop?

Stanford

Only by report, madame. A moneylender, is he not?

Lady Cheatly

He is a businessman. But that is only a small part of his life. He devotes most of his time to experiments in natural philosophy. He confidently expects to be elected to the Royal Society any day.

Stanford

Indeed?

Lady Cheatly

Come, it is time for his swimming lesson. I will show you.

(The scene opens to discover Scroop learning to swim upon a table. Trim and the Swimming Master are standing by.)

Trim

This is very fine; in a short time you will arrive at that perfection in this watery science that not a frog will exceed you.

Swimming Master

Ah, well struck, sir. That was admirable. That was as well swum as any man in England. Observe the frog, draw up your arms a little nearer and then thrust them out strongly. So—very well—incomparable.

Stanford

Let's not interrupt, madame, but observe a little this great curiosity.

Lady Cheatly.

It is a noble invention. A thing the Royal College never thought on.

Scroop

Let me rest a little to respire. So, it is wonderful, my noble friend, to observe the agility of this pretty animal, which notwithstanding I impede its motion by the detention of this filum or thread within my teeth, which makes a ligature about its loins and though by many sudden stops I cause the animal to sink—yet with indefatigable activity it rises upon the superficies of this humid element.

Trim

True, noble sir, and I am confident your genius will make art equal or exceed nature; nor will this or any other frog upon the face of the earth out swim you.

Scroop

(roused, enthusiastic) Sir, I expect, in a little time, to become amphibious; a man of art may appropriate any element to himself. I am now so far advanced in the art of flying that I can already out fly that ponderous animal called a hoot owl; nor should any greyhound in England catch me once I get upon wing.

Trim

Doubtless, sir, if you proceed in these swift gradations as you have in the past, you will no doubt succeed in your noble enterprise of flying to the moon.

Scroop

Right. For the moon being domina humidorum, to wit, the governess of moist bodies, it has, no doubt, the superior government of all islands.

(pause) Now, having sufficiently refreshed my lungs by way of respiration, I will return with renewed zeal to my swimming.

(Scroop lies back on the table and swims furiously.)

Swimming Master

Admirably well struck. Rarely swum. He shall swim with any man in Europe.

Trim

Hold sir, here is that noble gentleman I invited to kiss your hands. I am not a little proud of being the grateful and happy instrument of the necessitude and familiar communication which is like to intervene between you.

Stanford

Your most humble servant, sir.

Scroop

You are welcome to my poor laboratory.

Stanford

I am your humble admirer.

Trim

All the ingenious world are proud of Sir Nicholas Gimrack Scroop for his physico-mechanical excellencies.

Scroop

I confess I have some felicity in that way. Would my tongue were as rarely hung as yours and I would yield to none.

Stanford

Of all quaint inventions, none ever came near this of swimming.

Trim

An excellent method. In a fortnight it has advanced him to be the best swimmer in Europe. He can out-swim any fish of his size.

Stanford

Have you ever tried in the water, Mr. Scroop?

Scroop

Never, sir; but I swim most excellently on land. I hate water, sir. I never come upon water; it makes one confoundedly wet.

Stanford

Then, there is no use of swimming.

Scroop

I content myself with the speculative part of swimming; I care nothing for the practice. Like the Greeks, knowledge for its own sake is my ultimate end. But, I have begun a book on the subject.

(Enter Sir William.)

Stanford

Have you performed many experiments?

Scroop

Oh, yes. Most recently I transfused the blood of a sheep into a madman. The eminent sheep died.

Trim

Upon my integrity, he has advanced transfusion to the acme of perfection.

Scroop

The patient, from being manical became ovine or sheepish and chewed the cud; a sheep's tail soon emerged from his anus or human fundament.

Sir William

Will you never leave lying and quacking with your blood transfusions and fool's tricks? Why, if the blood of an ass were transfused into a virtuoso, you would not know the eminent ass from the recipient philosopher.

Trim

You are very pleasant and will have your jest.

Sir William

You are the zany to this mountebank.

Scroop

Cousin, don't interrupt us. To convince you of the truth of what I say, here's a letter from one of my patients who calls himself the meanest of my flock and sends me some of his own wool.

Sir William

Surely, he bleated his thanks to you. You deserve to be hanged. You killed four or five that I know of with your transfusions.

Scroop

(protesting) Their bowels were gangrened before the operation.

Sir William

All dead. And they hang murderers and cut purses while this quack walks free.

Scroop

I protest—

Sir William

Let me see you invent anything so useful as a mousetrap, and I'll believe some of your lies.

(Exit Sir William.)

Scroop

I hope you will pardon the rough nature of my cousin who spares nobody. By the way, gentlemen, what country air do you like best?

Stanford

Why, we cannot travel far for it this evening!

Scroop

Travel! Why, I never travel. I take it in a close chamber.

Stanford

How is this?

Scroop

Choose what air you like. Newmarket air, Bury air, Norwich air.

Stanford

But, how can you take several airs in your chamber?

Scroop

I employ men all over England who bottle up air, seal it hermetically, and send it to me.

Stanford

This is wondrous.

Scroop

Now I have a mind to Bury air.

(opening a cupboard, disclosing bottle after bottle) Help me open the bottles and be ready to snuff it up.

Trim

Isn't it admirable? Who would go to Bury to take it?

Scroop

Not I. It is much the fresher for being bottled.

Trim

(opening a bottle) 'Tis delicious. Very refreshing.

Scroop

Did I tell you I have it weighed? I can tell to a grain what a gallon of any air in England weighs.

Trim

The foolish world will soon learn to snuff up bottled air as they do bottled drink.

Scroop

That day, my fortune is made.

(Servant enters.)

Servant

Sir, sir! Stand upon your guard. The house is beset by a great rabble who threaten to pull you out of it and pull you to pieces.

Scroop

Heavens, what's the matter?

Servant

Sir, they are ribbon makers who have been informed you are the man who invented the engine loom and they are resolved to hang you for it, because they can get no work.

(Shouting without.)

Stanford

I shall be lucky to escape with my life for being in such company.

Faith, I deserve it.

Scroop

Gentlemen, gentlemen, I protest they wrong me. I never invented anything useful in my life.

Stanford

Get your guns and pistols charged.

Trim

Now it is time for me to show my parts. I have a better weapon.

Scroop

What weapon, Mr. Trim?

Trim

Eloquence. Let me alone, I shall calm the outrageous waters.

Stanford

Brave fool. It will never do.

Trim

You know not the charm of oratory. Not long ago it was my fortune to be near the Temple stairs when the water-men, having drunk too deep of liquor were blown into a tempest. Straight I ventured into the intemperate crowd, and by pouring honeyed words on the seas, calmed them, dispelled the barbarity of their overly fermented minds, and gently recomposed them into a sedate temper.

(going out heroically) Now, for the power of oratory.

Lady Cheatly

Protect me.

Scroop

Be so kind, sir, as to remain here with my sister. I shall take the precaution of backing Mr. Trim's honeyed words with muskets. Arm yourself, Roger.

(Exit Swimming Master, Scroop, and Servant, after Trim.)

Lady Cheatly

Do not think, sir, that just because we are alone that you can—

Stanford

Never dream of it.

Lady Cheatly

My honor is proof against such chances, I assure you.

Stanford

I would never.

Lady Cheatly

If your intentions be not honorable, you'll provoke me strangely.

Stanford

Madame, I assure you—

Lady Cheatly

I am experienced and proof against (softly) temptation.

Stanford

(aside) 'Sdeath. She will talk of nothing else.

(Enter Emilia.)

Lady Cheatly

(stamping her foot) What makes you saucily intrude on this gentleman and me?

Emilia

A certain curiosity of doing things that are forbidden me.

Lady Cheatly

'Tis very well. But, pray you gape not after him. You may, if you please, call him uncle. In the meantime, get you in.

(aside) Will the slut forage with her mother? She shall have none of him!

(Emilia leaves as she came. Voices are heard from the crowd.)

Voices

Hang the fop. Kill the word monger. Death to the virtuoso.

(A volley of gunshots. Lady Cheatly huddles against Stanford. The servant returns.)

Servant

Sir Positive Atall and Mr. Prig dispersed the mob with gunfire. They had nearly lynched Mr. Trim.

Stanford

Oh, now I am undone and ruined forever. Sir Positive is coming.

(Enter Prig and Positive, to the confusion of Lady Cheatly. Servant leaves.)

Sir Positive

I heard your ladyship was here and came to kiss your hand.

(spying Stanford who was trying to hide in a corner) Oh, Stanford, you here. Well, I am glad you are together. You shall hear the music I promised you this morning.

Stanford

Let it be another time. (aside) When shall I be delivered from these fools?

Sir Positive

(looking at his music) Let me see. Fa, la, la.

Stanford

Sure this is magic never to be free.

Sir Positive

Do you talk of magic?

Stanford

No, no, no, not I. I understand nothing of it.

Sir Positive

I do. If you please, talk of something else, leave that to me.

Prig

Dear Stanford, I knew I would find you here. I had not the power to stay away. Let me hug you, dear heart.

(embracing the horrified Stanford) I had rather hug you than any woman.

Lady Cheatly

For the honor of our sex, pray you remain of the same mind.

Prig

I'll tell you, dear heart, I love you with all my heart. You're a man of sense. I am infinitely happy in your friendship, for between you and me this town is more pestered with idle fellows than you can imagine.

Stanford

I have every reason to believe you.

Prig

(drawing him aside) But, I have a secret to impart to you.

Stanford

(hastily) Don't trust me with it. I have a faculty of telling all I know. I cannot help of it.

Prig

Only this, Stanford. I have heard your resolution to quit this town. I am of your opinion. It's intolerable that you can never be free from fools in this town. I like your resolution so well that I am the son of a whore if I don't go along with you.

Stanford

(aghast) You honor me too much.

Prig

I always stand by my friends.

Lady Cheatly

I think retiring to a monastery is very poetic.

Prig

Very.

Lady Cheatly

It puts me in mind of Mr. Trim's poetry.

Prig

(acidly) Trim, a poet? A poetical pimp, is he not?

Sir Positive

(looking up from his music) Who's that speaks of pimping? Well! But, I cannot pass this without manifest injury to myself.

Lady Cheatly

But, sir, are you such a man?

Sir Positive

Why, madame, did you never hear of me for this?

Lady Cheatly

No, sir—if I had—

Sir Positive

If you had! Ha, ha, ha. Why, where have you lived all this while?

Lady Cheatly

(upset) I shall lose my precious reputation if I be seen in his company.

Sir Positive

The pimps in this town are a company of empty, idle, insipid, dull fellows that have no design in them.

Lady Cheatly

I am sorry you are such a man.

Sir Positive

Sorry! If I were to apply myself to it, I would starve all these pimps.

Lady Cheatly

Surely, you are jesting?

Sir Positive

Jesting? Why, there is not a whore in this entire town that I am not intimately acquainted with, that I do not know the state of her body from first entering into her calling.

Lady Cheatly

Sir!

Sir Positive

Besides, for debauching women, madame, I am the greatest whoremaster in the British Isles, nay, Europe, too.

Lady Cheatly

Out upon you! If you be such a man, I will never see you more.

(aside) Is it possible he is such a man? It's easy to underestimate people.

Sir Positive

I beg a thousand pardons. I was speaking only of the speculative part of pimping, not the practical.

Lady Cheatly

(aside, disappointed) I knew it all along.

(aloud) If you had not brought yourself off with your speculation, I would never have suffered you to have practiced on me. No woman in England values her honor more than I do.

(Enter Steward.)

Steward

Your daughters request your presence, and the presence of the gentlemen.

Lady Cheatly

Gentlemen, if you will go in, I have a collation prepared—and cards. I will present my daughters to you. I must have a word with my Steward.

(The gentlemen leave.)

Lady Cheatly

How many mortgages have I got today?

Steward

Three, madame, and the prospect of three more.

Lady Cheatly

Excellent. (she begins to go in)

Steward

Madame, I have private business for your ladyship's ear.

Lady Cheatly

Speak freely.

Steward

My business concerns your ladyship and myself so nearly that you must pardon me if I urge it home.

Lady Cheatly

Speak plainly.

Steward

You yourself can witness that I've served you faithfully.

Lady Cheatly

I can and I'll reward you well.

Steward

In your service, I have lost my honesty, betrayed my conscience, and become an accessory to your frauds.

Lady Cheatly

I am sorry you think it necessary to ask for the reward I intended to give you. You may take a thousand pounds. That's generous, I hope.

Steward

A thousand pounds. A paltry thousand pounds. I scorn it.

Lady Cheatly

You scorn it?

Steward

The bonds you have given to people and the assignments and declaration of trust you have given your brother are worthless. They are written in a special ink that I myself procured for you and within a month will vanish. Is it not true?

Lady Cheatly

What then? My husband was cheated of his estate by my brother and 'tis fit I should take letters of reprisal.

Steward

(dryly) No doubt.

Lady Cheatly

(uneasily) When my estate is out of dispute, you may have more and gladly!

Steward

I do not desire money.

Lady Cheatly

Then, why this blackmailing?

Steward

No, madame, I have long honored and loved you. Nothing less than your person can ever satisfy me.

Lady Cheatly

How, sir!

Steward

Take care, madame. Be not proud. Be not haughty. With one word I can blast your fortune and send you to Newgate. But, marry me, and I'll be your humble servant as before.

Lady Cheatly

Insolent villain. Surely you are jesting?

Steward

By heaven, it is no jest.

Lady Cheatly

Give me time to consider of it.

Steward

I can give none, nor will.

Lady Cheatly

Marriage will stop all my business and I shall get no more money from my brother.

Steward

We'll keep it private.

Lady Cheatly

(sweetly) I must confess, it is the thing I wished for most upon earth.

Steward

(ecstatic) Then, I am happy and will serve you till my death.

Lady Cheatly

(aside) Which may be soon!

(embracing him) Now we understand each other. One difficulty remains. You are my main witness and when we are married you cannot be a witness; therefore, if you will go to a Master of Chancery and swear to all my deeds and make an affidavit to my estate, the next hour shall make me your wife.

Steward

(smiling) Before, Madame, I never will. After, for my own sake, I must. I shall not be your dupe, madame.

Lady Cheatly

But, if it is found we are married—

Steward

I shall procure a parson and none shall know it but him.

Lady Cheatly

On the condition that I procure the parson myself, I agree.

Steward

I am transported with happiness.

Lady Cheatly

(aside) You shall be transported indeed if you are lucky enough not to be hanged. (aloud) My brother is coming. Withdraw, I'll come to you as soon as I can.

(The Steward goes out. Enter Scroop by another door.)

Scroop

Well, sister, it takes.

Lady Cheatly

(uneasily) I told you it would. Where are there more fools than in London?

Scroop

You shall not want money so long as I have deeds of trust from you. All London thinks you are fabulously wealthy.

Lady Cheatly

Some pious old fellow will snap at me, and the rash young fools at my daughters.

Scroop

I wish you would go to church. It might be a great advantage. I myself have made much benefit of religion; it is a pious fraud and very lawful.

Lady Cheatly

No, brother. The Godly have two qualities which would hinder my design: great covetousness (which would make them pry too narrowly into my fortune) and much eating (which would eat up what I have).

Scroop

Reproach not the Godly, sister. But, I warn you. Have a care of the wits. Wits are good for nothing.

Lady Cheatly

They value pleasure and will bid high for it.

Scroop

They understand not business.

Lady Cheatly

All the better.

Scroop

I fear you are vilely tainted with wit.

(Steward enters.)

Steward

The scriveners are come, madame.

Lady Cheatly

Excellent. Bid them wait.

Scroop

I must visit my wife.

(Exit Scroop.)

Steward

Your design prospers beyond our hopes. It has taken fire like a train. All believe yours to be a great fortune. The belief in your wealth has spread so far that two citizens from Dublin have just applied to me to trust their money into your hands, believing you can employ to more advantage than anybody.

Lady Cheatly

You did not refuse them?

Steward

They will bring their money in the morning. They had to bribe me to get me to take it.

Lady Cheatly

Ha, ha, ha! And men fancy they understand business.

Steward

Do not forget our agreement.

Lady Cheatly

It is on my mind. But you must be patient, I have guests.

(They confer at one side of the room. Enter Mr. Scroop, bringing in his wife by the arm.)

Mrs. Scroop

Will this tyranny never end? Must I always be thus abridged of liberty? A cooped-up chicken is well fed, but I am cooped up and starved.

Scroop

Come, love, you have very good, wholesome food. Besides, it's fit that a young woman should mortify her flesh to keep down her lusts.

Mrs. Scroop

In winter I am kept without fire or candle.

Scroop

To preserve your life, my love. Did you ever see a long-lived cook? Fire destroys natural heat.

Mrs. Scroop

In winter, your servants wish the plague or any hot disease. For my part, I could be contented with a mere fever.

Scroop

Could you not exercise to stir up your natural heat?

Mrs. Scroop

You give me little enough exercise, heaven knows.

Scroop

(placatingly) Sweet.

(aside) I knew it was exercise she wants.

Mrs. Scroop

I have endured your cruel tyranny too long. But, above all, your jealousy is most provoking.

Scroop

It's nothing but my love, my great love. I look upon you as I do my money. I know what a treasure you are.

Mrs. Scroop

I'll have the liberty of an Englishwoman.

Scroop

What? The liberty of receiving visits and meeting young whoremasters—of cuckolding your husband?

Mrs. Scroop

(defiantly) If it pleases me.

Scroop

Go to your room, hussy.

Mrs. Scroop

(venomously) I will be quits with you.

Scroop

No, you shall not. I will take care not to be a cuckold.

Mrs. Scroop

(aside) Not care enough.

(aloud) Peace, old fool. You have worn out all my patience. Henceforward, I will be a tigress to you. Know, old man, I have a twin brother, a captain in the army, who will right me. There is no fiercer man in all England. He'll cut your throat if you abuse me.

Scroop

You threaten me with your brother?

Mrs. Scroop

I will have fifty pounds a night to gamble with.

Scroop

Fifty pounds, dear God.

Mrs. Scroop

Does it break your heart? I'll make you know the right of an Englishwoman before I have done.

Scroop

Then, correction will ensue.

(Scroop lifts his cane to her. Mrs. Scroop wrests it out of his hand.)

Servant

(entering) Sir, your cousin Sir Humphrey Blockhead-Swash is just entering with a great train of gentlemen and ladies and has sent a collation of wine that you may not be at charges.

Lady Cheatly

Lewd wretch. I have forbidden him the house.

Scroop

Confound him and his train. Do you hear, Mrs. go into your chamber.

Mrs. Scroop

I will stay to entertain the ladies.

Scroop

Ladies? Whores! In, or this knife shall be imbrued in thy blood.

Mrs. Scroop

(defiantly) I will not go in.

(Enter Sir Humphrey, Sir Christopher, Bluffe, Hackum, Tope, Lucy, Striker and Friske with fiddlers.)

Sir Humphrey

What's the matter, at wars with your wife, cousin?

Scroop

My dear wife! No, she is not well, she will endanger her health; and something else which is quite dear to me.

Mrs. Scroop

I am very well. I shall not endanger my health, nor is it dear to him. Ladies, your humble servant. I am proud of the honor of this visit.

(All the company "salute," that is kiss, Mrs. Scroop and Lady Cheatly.)

Scroop

Ounds! She can compliment. Death. They kiss most lasciviously.

Sir Humphrey

Oh, my sweet, my honored cousin Lady Cheatly, your humble servant. It is a common blockheaded trick to serenade and disturb people at midnight, I am come to serenade you at nine. I come a housewarming.

Lady Cheatly

Unheard of impudence. Did I not forbid you my house?

Sir Humphrey

Look you, cousin, if you will be civil and well-bred, I will kiss your hand and use you like a relation. But if wars must ensue, I will roar and scour your house so that you might lie as quietly in a besieged town with bombs and carcasses flying about your lodging.

Lady Cheatly

Avaunt, devil incarnate. I'll order you.

Sir Humphrey

Then, enter my friend Jack Tope, all my singers, fiddlers and whole equipage. Strike up, my lads.

Tope

Come on, my boys, halloo. Come lady, give me your hand, dance and frisk about.

Lady Cheatly

Hang this old coxcomb.

(to Sir Humphrey) Sir, I hope you will be so civil as to leave my house and to take that old sinner with you.

Tope

(indignantly) No older a sinner than yourself. For serenading and scouring, have at you, dear lady.

Sir Christopher

(to Scroop) How dost thou do, old boy? We are come to drink, sing, and be merry with you.

(singing) The king's most faithful subjects we, In his service are not dull. We drink to show our loyalty, And make his coffers full. Would all his subjects drink like us, We'd make him richer far, More powerful and more prosperous, Than all the Eastern monarchs are, Than all the Eastern monarchs are.

Sir Humphrey

(to Mrs. Scroop) To show you I bear you no ill will from this morning, I will endeavor your release. Be ready.

Mrs. Scroop

You oblige me.

Scroop

(coming between them) Have you any private business with my wife?

Sir Christopher

What a pox! Do you interrupt a gentleman that's talking to your wife?

Bluffe

He deserves chastisement, uncivil old prig.

Hackum

If he had offered that to me, I would have blown him into atoms.

Sir Christopher

Shall I beat him and kick him damnably and break all his windows, ha?

Sir Humphrey

Not yet. Come, ladies. I have brought my fiddles. Let's dance.

Scroop

What will become of me? Hell is broke loose. Housewife, remember this.

(to Sir Humphrey) No, sir, I thank you.

(to servant) Go for the constable.

Servant

Not for the world. Here's a bumper to his health.

Scroop

Hell and confusion! Rogue, I'll murder you.

Servant

But, you shall not starve me more, as long as Sir Humphrey lives.

(The dancing has begun. Sir Humphrey leads Mrs. Scroop.)

Mrs. Scroop

Perfidious man. How I long to tear your eyes out.

Sir Humphrey

You always had a tender heart.

Scroop

Ounds! She dances. Now, where did that slut learn to dance?

(The dancing continues.)

Lady Cheatly

(to Scroop) Tame beast. Make a warrant and send them to the gatehouse or to Newgate. Oh, what a pitiful nincompoop. What, do you fear him?

Scroop

Have a little patience. I must secure my wife.

Tope

Consider, madame, patience is a great virtue for a lady of your years.

Lady Cheatly

My years! I spit at you, you old rascal. My years!

Tope

You are a notable girl.

Lady Cheatly

(yelling) Begone, you villainous, lewd rascals.

Tope

Strike up. Louder. Out noise her.

(The music plays louder.)

Lady Cheatly

Ruffians, vagabonds, ragamuffins, slaves, dogs, scoundrels, hold, hold, hold!

(Stanford enters from the house and goes to Lady Cheatly.)

Stanford

Dissemble a little, madame.

Lady Cheatly

Well, you have silenced me.

(to Sir Humphrey) I shall not object since you say you intend but a little civil music.

Scroop

(seeing Sir Humphrey leading out Mrs. Scroop) Hell and devils. What trick is this? Oh, my wife, my wife!

(Scroop rushes in to grab her.)

Sir Humphrey

Are you mad? It's part of the dance.

Scroop

You shall lead her no such dance.

Sir Christopher

What, do you interrupt the dance? I'll maul you. (kicking Scroop)

Mrs. Scroop

Excellent. I'd give two hundred pounds for this. Taming of the senses with a vengeance.

Sir Humphrey

Fill every brimmer to Mrs. Scroop's health. Give Scroop one.

Sir Christopher

(to Scroop) Take it and drink to your lady's health or, by the devil, I will mortify your old flesh.

Scroop

Curses. Well, there's no remedy. (drinking)

Sir Christopher

Well, cousin Humphrey, am I not a very mad fellow?

Scroop

Gentlemen, what have I done to deserve these outrages?

Sir Christopher

Done? Damme, you are a rogue and a usurer and a virtuoso. Is that not enough?

Striker

Done! Filthy fellow, to shut up your wife against the law of nature.

Sir Humphrey

(to Lady Cheatly) I must have both my cousins, your daughters. It is my intention to welcome them to town.

Lady Cheatly

Out of my house. You shall be hanged first.

Sir Humphrey

Secure the doors! Let nobody out. Come lads, let's march and roar. I will search every room in the house, but I will have them.

Tope

We knights errant, lady, are bound by our noble order to succor distressed damsels and free them from enchanted castles and from your viragos, madame, your viragos.

Stanford

(to Sir Humphrey) You shall not carry this off. I passed my word to Lady Cheatly to protect her, and I shall require a strict account of this affront you have put upon her.

Sir Humphrey

Are you concerned with the honor of my cousin? What, do you lie with her?

Stanford

What say you, sir?

Lady Cheatly

Foul-mouthed brute, hold! Shall I, who am as notorious for my virtue as for my wealth, be blasted by your contagious breath?

Sir Humphrey

What, I? Heaven forbid that I might blast your honor with my breath.

(whistling and walking away) What, my saintly cousin? Why, I love and honor thee.

Lady Cheatly

Love and honor me? Pray, love and honor me and civilly get out of my house.

Sir Humphrey

I will, in good time. But, by this hand, I will serenade thee most confoundedly.

Lady Cheatly

(to Stanford) Sir, I must have your word not to quarrel with him. No dueling.

Stanford

Have no fear, there will be no duel.

(Stanford and Sir Humphrey speak apart.)

Sir Humphrey

Well acted. It goes according to our plan. (to the company) Let us dance again, Mrs. Scroop.

(Another dance is played.)

Scroop

Come back, whoremaster! Have I caught you, strumpet? There is a law, sir, remember that.

Hackum

Does the scoundrel talk of law?

Bluffe

Beat his brains out.

Mrs. Scroop

No, gentlemen. He is an old man, and even though he shuts me up in prison—

Friske and Striker

How, shut up your wife?

Striker

Thou old dotard! Thou shame of mankind.

Friske

Woman was meant to go at large. Filthy creature.

Sir Humphrey

He invades the right of whoremasters.

Lady Cheatly

Promise me you have not fixed a duel.

Stanford

Indeed, no, dear lady. Promise to meet me— (he whispers)

Lady Cheatly

Must it be so?

Sir Humphrey

(to Mrs. Scroop) I have a sure way to free you and my cousins.

(whispers to Tope) Douse the lights!

(All the lights go out.)

Scroop

Help. Murder. Villains. I am cuckolded, robbed. Whoremasters, strumpets.

Lady Cheatly

(to Stanford) Come now, come quickly. I will hid you, then I will come to you.

Stanford

At once, dear lady.

(Stanford and Lady Cheatly steal out.)

Sir Humphrey

(to Tope) Count to ten, then yell "fire." Be sure to set one, too.

Mrs. Scroop

Where are you, my dear? I am sorry if I've been a bad girl. (leading Striker to him and giving him her hand)

Scroop

That's a girl. Take Daddy's hand.

(aside) I'll break all the harlot's bones.

(Tope, Hackum, Bluffe, and Sir Christopher all yell "Fire, fire, fire.")

Mrs. Scroop

(exiting) And now, farewell.

(The women shriek.)

Hackum

Gad, it's dark. Have at these women.

(Hackum kisses Friske. Bluffe strikes him.)

Bluffe

Hands off.

Hackum

What rascal cuffed me? Have at somebody.

Sir Humphrey

(drawing) What's the matter?

(All the men draw, the women shriek. A brawl ensues.)

Sir Christopher

Fight on, merry men.

Hackum

Blood will ensue.

Scroop

(leading Striker) Now, madame, I shall chastise you for your insolence, your whorishness.

Striker

(cuffing him) I don't play that game, old fool.

Scroop

Who is this? My wife, my wife! Where is my wife?

Lady Cheatly

(returning in a fury) Damn you. You spiritless wretch. They have got my daughters out of the house. Tomorrow, into the country they go. I'll order them.

Tope

Come along, my lads, Hem, hem, madame. Now you shall see who's old. I will be master of the revels. Ah, I see you have a lady, Mr. Scroop. Come, join the dance.

ACT II
SCENE 6

A Room in Scroop's house later that night.

Stanford is waiting for Lady Cheatly. She enters with her fingers to her lips, hushing Stanford.

Stanford

Sweet madame, your ladyship is come much earlier than I expected. Let me secure the door.

(Stanford goes to the door, slipping out and letting Tope in.)

Lady Cheatly

Sweet sir, you deserve to be trusted by a lady. (aside) It's useless trying to pursue my daughters; I have sent the Steward after them to keep him busy. Well, it's an ill wind that doesn't blow some good. Ah, you're returning, my Adonis.

(Lady Cheatly does not look around and Tope embraces her from behind.)

Tope

My dear, dear—

Lady Cheatly

(recognizing the voice and struggling to free herself) Who's there? Old Satan!

Tope

I thought you had been past the age of squeaking.

Lady Cheatly

(trying to get loose) Devil, how came you here?

Tope

Sweet lady, how came you here?

Lady Cheatly

Abused, betrayed, undone. They shall not live who have done this.

Tope

Oh, madame, ladies should kill but with their eyes. Men of honor assist one another in these necessities.

Lady Cheatly

Vile pimp. Pimp for you.

Tope

Pimp is a foul word. Pimps are rogues. Men of honor are gentlemen.

Lady Cheatly

(struggling in great fury) If only I had a dagger. Let me go, old decrepit nincompoop.

Tope

Not so old as all that. I shall convince you by and by. Have at you.

Lady Cheatly

Help, help, murder!

Tope

You squeak like one sixteen. If only you could look so. Come, sweet madame, let us be more familiar.

(undoing his breeches)

Lady Cheatly

Stand off, you driveling drunkard. I'll scratch your eyes out.

Tope

Sweet lady, I can secure my eyes against your hands. Ah, could I have defended my poor heart but half so well against your eyes.

Lady Cheatly

(softly) Let go my hands.

Tope

Let go my heart.

Lady Cheatly

(very softly) Help, help. A rape.

(Tope opens the door and he and Lady Cheatly go out together. A slight pause. Enter Miranda and Trim.)

Trim

Now, if your love has any resolution, you may enjoy me and make yourself the happiest lady in town—and please me, too.

Miranda

You are so well-bred, so much a gentleman, that all the ladies must love you.

Trim

(complacently) It's true.

Miranda

(fondling his lace) And then, you dress so finely.

Trim

Most young fellows, when they come to town, attempt to imitate my dress. But, pretty creature, let us retire.

Miranda

What you please, sir, if you will be civil.

Trim

How she adores me.

(Miranda and Trim go out together.)

Miranda's voice

But, do you love me?

Trim's voice

I kiss the hem of your petticoat.

(Prig enters and, hearing the voices, follows them off, looking indignant. Enter Sir William and Friske.)

Sir William

How happy I am to have found you here, love.

Friske

Dearest, come to me. No one will bother us here.

Sir William

You are a dear creature. It's a wicked age; men these days are without conscience or respect. In Cromwell's time, men were modest and ladies virtuous.

Friske

I blush at the impudent creatures of this town. That's the truth of it.

Sir William

So do I. To see villains wrong their wives, while spending money on strumpets. It makes my heart bleed.

Friske

Filthy wenches, I am amazed they dare to show their faces.

Sir William

The young are worse. Look at my son and Sir Humphrey. Nothing but swearing, drinking and whoring. I should be weary of the world and its vices but that you comfort me sometimes.

Friske

Talk no more of them. I spit at them. Kiss me.

Sir William

(fondling her) Poor sweetheart. Poor darling! We are civil now. What harm's in this?

Friske

None. None. Poor dear, kiss me again.

Sir William

Poor thing, you shall have this purse.

Friske

I love you, not money. I cannot abide money.

(she takes the purse and it disappears into her clothing) But, if you wish it, to please you.

Sir William

Poor little thing. I'll bite you on the lips. You have incensed me strangely; you have fired my blood. I can bear it no longer Where are the instruments of our pleasure?

Friske

Our pleasure?

Sir William

(imperiously) Do not frown. You shall do it now.

Friske

I wonder that should please you so much that pleases me so little.

Sir William

I was so used to it at school, I could never leave it off since.

Friske

Well, if I must.

(Friske looks about and finds some birch rods.)

Sir William

(pulling down his breeches) But, you are too gentle. You must be stern! Stern! I have been a bad boy. Spare the rod and spoil the child.

Hackum

(outside) Open the door, you slut. What rascal have you got with you?

Friske

(scared) It's my brother.

Sir William

(pulling up his pants) Hectoring rascal. We had none of this in the last age. Rogues! Dogs! A man cannot be private with a sister, but he must be disturbed by an impertinent brother.

Hackum

(bursting in) Where is the slut? By God, it's the young squire's father.

Sir William

Rogue! Dog! Where is my son? I'll cut your throat.

Hackum

(stunned) With his breeches down. Wait till I tell Sir Christopher.

Sir William

(helplessly) I WAS TRYING TO FIND MY SON.

Hackum

With your breeches down? Ho, ho, ho.

Sir William

I'll kill you, you dog.

(Chasing after Hackum with his sword in one hand and holding up his breeches with the other.)

Friske

I must think of something to say to Sir Christopher. How was I to know the old goat was his father?

(Friske rushes out. Sounds of cursing off. Enter Prig and Trim.)

Prig

You have debauched Miss Miranda.

Trim

She debauched me, sir.

Prig

Come, come, have you made your will?

Trim

Yes, yes, don't trouble yourself for that. I have it always ready upon these occasions.

Prig

If you have not, your estate may be divided by the lawyers after I have killed you.

Trim

Sweet Mr. Prig, don't think to frighten me, for I am the son of a rhinoceros if I fear you more than I do a chipmunk.

Prig

Under favor, I will run you through the lungs immediately.

Trim

I am no gentleman if I don't stick you to the ground at the first pass.

Prig

Have at you.

(Trim and Prig fight. Trim wins.)

Trim

No, pray quickly.

Prig

I cannot pray very well, but...I can run. (running off)

Trim

(running after him) Are you so nimble? I shall overtake you.

(Trim cannot catch Prig) Surely this rogue has run the marathon.

(Enter Mrs. Striker.)

Trim

Hold, hold, I say. I'll spare your life two minutes while I wait upon this lady.

Prig

Spare my life! I scorn your words. But, take leave of her, since it is the last time you will ever see her, after I tell her what you have done with Miss Miranda.

Trim

Vile devil! Will you ruin me with both my mistresses?

(to Striker) Madame, I will but run this fellow through the body a little, and I'll walk you home.

(to Prig) Stand your ground, you coxcomb. Do you think I am bound to fight you by the mile?

(Striker runs off shrieking.)

Prig

Let's stay a little and debate this business over a bottle of wine.

Trim

No more words, I am roused, I am angry, I am ready.

Prig

Look you, dear Trim, the case is this—

Trim

(chasing Prig) Will you never give over?

Prig

We must adjourn the combat. It's too dark in here. We cannot see to kill each other. I have sworn never to fight when I cannot see to parry.

Trim

Light some candles.

Prig

(retreating) I have thought it over. Trim, you're a very honest fellow. I have an affection for you and devil take me if I will fight with you.

Trim

Why did you call me out then?

Prig

Very rash of me, I confess. Upon my honor, I'll give you a diamond ring and my favorite horse if you'll oblige me in one thing.

Trim

What can it be?

Prig

Pretend you fought with me and disarmed me.

Trim

I already did.

Prig

Exactly. All we need to do is to make it look a little more convincing.

Trim

This is strange.

Prig

I'll do as much for you upon any occasion. Upon my honor.

Trim

Would you have a gentleman lie for you?

Prig

Why, I'll lie for you again, man, when you will. What do you talk of that? Here, take my ring. Do it.

(Trim takes the ring.)

Trim

Very well. But there must be some sign of blood.

Prig

How shall we contrive that?

(worried) Wouldn't it be better just to tear my shirt a little?

Trim

Take your sword and run yourself through the arm.

Prig

Thank you for that! I've known men to have died of that.

Trim

I'll do it myself, then.

Prig

(flinching) Hold, hold, you may prick an artery and I'll bleed to death. You don't want to be hanged, do you? It will be as well if my shirt be bloody at the hand. I'll prick my finger for that and run through my coat.

Trim

Oh, do as you will.

Prig

Dear Trim, kiss me. You have obliged me so! If I die without issue, I'll make you my heir.

(Enter Sir Positive.)

Sir Positive

What's this? Swords drawn. Put up, for shame. Put up. I am afraid you do not understand these nice points of honor.

Prig

He had the insolence to call me a dog.

Trim

And he called me a son of a bitch.

Sir Positive

You are out! See the fault of men's education. Why, if any man tells you more about honor, I am the son of a squirrel. Upon my honor, you shall embrace.

(Sir Positive leads them out, expostulating to them. Enter Emilia and Stanford.)

Emilia

Well, I am sure I am very foolish to see you like this. I put it down to my desire to avoid Sir Positive.

Stanford

I doubt I should have come, but I feared to meet Mr. Trim.

Emilia

(trying the door) We are locked in.

Stanford

They must intend to make us as troublesome to each other as they are to us.

Emilia

(aside) He's so agreeable. I could listen to him all day. (aloud) They intend to shut us up like a jury until we agree.

Stanford

That will be longer than the siege of Troy. If you become troublesome, I shall break down the door to escape.

(aside) I could look at her until dawn.

Emilia

Why don't you break open the door?

Stanford

(sighing) I don't find much reason for it yet.

Emilia

I could find it in my heart to give you enough.

Stanford

Undoubtedly, madame, it is in your nature.

(the key turns in the lock) Someone has unlocked the door, I think.

Emilia

Why don't you go? The door is open now, sir.

Stanford

I am afraid I shall light on worse company.

Emilia

Oh, sir, that's impossible.

Stanford

How vain this is of you. Now you would give me occasion to flatter you, but I assure you, you will miss in your design.

Emilia

Well, this is an extraordinary man. I love the very sight of him.

(aloud) I wonder, sir, you'll be so foppish as to imagine I love to be flattered.

Stanford

What an owl I am to like this woman. Sure, I am bewitched.

(aloud) Why don't you leave, madame?

Emilia

(offering to go) I will. Yet, I'd rather stay here than venture out. You are not so insupportable.

Stanford

(aside) Rare woman.

(Enter Sir Positive.) Good God, Sir Positive. It is too late to fly.

Sir Positive

Do you talk of flying, Jack? I'll teach you that with the greatest ease in the world.

(Emilia and Stanford exchange a significant glance, as the Curtain falls.)

CURTAIN

ACT III
SCENE 7

Sir Humphrey's house, early next morning. It is evident that there has been an orgy. Bottles and litter are everywhere.

Enter Mrs. Scroop, dressed as her brother Captain Wildfire; she wears a sword and carries a swagger stick.

Mrs. Scroop

I see that this is a fine well-governed household.

Tope

(starting up from the couch where he has been sleeping) Hush, captain, the servants are all drunk and asleep.

Mrs. Scroop

I must speak with Sir Humphrey Blockhead-Swash. My business is urgent.

Tope

I'll find him. Halloo, brother! You have a visitor.

(Enter Sir Humphrey in a dressing gown, much the worse for

wear.)

Mrs. Scroop

I hope you will excuse the disturbance when you know my business.

Sir Humphrey

A gentleman's commands can never disturb me.

Mrs. Scroop

I am Harry Wildfire, brother to Letitia Scroop, wife of a wretched usurer, who, I am informed, is in your house.

Sir Humphrey

Yes, he brought the watch here, and was taken prisoner. I have him in the wine cellar. But you are much like your sister. Much like.

Mrs. Scroop

(aside) Oh, how I long to scratch his face. But I have a better way.

(aloud) We are as much alike as it is possible to be, sir. If her husband is here, I beg you will deliver him over to me to be used as he deserves for the barbarity he has practiced on my sister.

Sir Humphrey

Nothing would please me better. My house is free to you. Sir, I will go in and dress and then wait on you.

(Exit Sir Humphrey and Tope. Pause. Tope leads in a bedraggled Scroop.)

Mrs. Scroop

Is your name Scroop?

Scroop

It is.

(looking at Wildfire) You look damnably like my wife.

Mrs. Scroop

I am Wildfire, her brother. I have been at her house and she is missing.

Scroop

Missing? The slut has not returned home?

Mrs. Scroop

Murderer. You have killed her. I am here to take revenge.

Scroop

She has run away from me, and I believe she is in this house, playing the whore with Sir Humphrey.

Mrs. Scroop

Villain, you lie! Upon my honor, you have not a quarter of an hour to live. Had she not been murdered, she would have come to one of her relations.

Scroop

(leaving) If she be killed, I had no hand in it.

Mrs. Scroop

(striking him with her swagger stick) Would you try to leave? Try again.

Scroop

(rubbing his shoulder) I wasn't going anywhere at all.

Mrs. Scroop

Kneel and pray.

Scroop

I cannot pray.

Mrs. Scroop

The damned never can. I have lost a sister, and unless you produce her this instant, I shall do my country and all your debtors a service by sacrificing your life.

Scroop

Let me settle my affairs. If you kill me, you will deprive the world of one of the greatest natural philosophers of the age.

Mrs. Scroop

What do I care about natural philosophy? No. You must die now.

Scroop

On the word of a dying man, your sister ran away from me. I locked her up to save the honor of your family, for she is a most salacious woman.

Mrs. Scroop

My sister? Salacious? Do you insult my sister?

Scroop

I only said—

Mrs. Scroop

You insult the memory of my sister, old dotard?

(drawing) Die now.

Scroop

Let me but live to repent a while.

Mrs. Scroop

Dissuade me not.

(Enter Sir Humphrey, dressed.)

Sir Humphrey

Do not kill him.

Mrs. Scroop

What use is there to let him live?

Scroop

I am but fifty years old, sir. But fifty years old.

Mrs. Scroop

Fifty years too old.

Sir Humphrey

Hear me, good captain. He seems to me to be a sturdy old bird that can carry arms.

Mrs. Scroop

Say you so? Ay, that will do. I'll take him as a recruit to Flanders. And if I don't hear of my sister in a reasonable time, I'll hang him or put him before a firing squad.

Scroop

But, noble captain, I am a hideous coward. I shall run away.

Mrs. Scroop

Do! And I shall have the distinct pleasure of hanging you according to the law. Here, take a shilling, usurer.

Scroop

I must confess, I have a great respect for a shilling and never could refuse one in my life.

Mrs. Scroop

You are enrolled, sir.

Scroop

(cunningly) I hope you'll let me go upon parole, sir, to furnish myself with necessaries.

Mrs. Scroop

No, I'll furnish them. If you run from your colors, soldier, I'll hang you by law.

Scroop

I'll give you fifty pounds to set me at liberty.

Mrs. Scroop

Give me the money, sir.

Scroop

(reluctantly) Here.

Mrs. Scroop

You are witness, Sir Humphrey. This recruit has attempted to bribe an officer of His Majesty to release him.

Sir Humphrey

I saw it and I heard it, sir.

Mrs. Scroop

He'll hang.

Scroop

Give me back my money.

Mrs. Scroop

Dog! The money is crown evidence. Do you lock him back in the cellar.

(Tope takes Scroop out. Enter Prig and Trim, who bow to Sir Humphrey. He acknowledges them curtly.)

Sir Humphrey

(to Mrs. Scroop) I have often heard of your worth and am glad of the opportunity of doing you a service. If you have a mind to a handsome wench, you shall have her.

Mrs. Scroop

There's no ill proposal; you shall find me a man at arms at all points.

(aside) Hold temper.

(Enter Lucy, Striker, and Friske.)

Sir Humphrey

Here is my mistress—her, I bar—but, the other tow, if you can win them, do.

Mrs. Scroop

Faith, I'll try. (kissing all the ladies)

Prig

I don't like these proceedings; this effeminate officer will be too hard for us.

Trim

Oh, wenches love an officer almost as much as a beau.

Lucy

(to Sir Humphrey) My dear, I have a lawyer ready for that settlement you were pleased to promise me. Not that I desire it, for while you live, I desire nothing else—but in the case of mortality. It will do me little good, for I shall scarce outlive you.

Sir Humphrey

I have promised, and a Blockhead–Swash is a man of his word. Come.

(Lucy and Sir Humphrey exit.)

Prig

Let's observe how this captain fares with our wenches.

Striker

He's the prettiest man ever born.

Friske

You cannot have been long a solder, you're so young and (caressing him) you face is so (softly) smooth.

Striker

How do the women in Flanders do it?

Mrs. Scroop

Do it?

Striker

You know, make love.

(Mrs. Scroop whispers in her ear.)

Striker

(giggling) Really? I've never tried that.

Friske

And our brave soldiers, how do they fare?

Mrs. Scroop

Well enough, if they strike home briskly. (kissing both of them)

Striker

Brisk, indeed. Would Mr. Trim were half so brisk.

Friske

You're a good-natured man. Have you been in many battles?

Mrs. Scroop

Many. And I have stormed many fortresses, too.

Striker

And did you rape many women?

Mrs. Scroop

More than I can count.

Friske

I'm sure it was unnecessary.

Mrs. Scroop

(to Striker) My time is short and I wish I were rid of her. I am much taken with you.

Striker

(delighted) Flatterer.

Friske

Captain, a word in your ear.

Mrs. Scroop

(to Friske) Pretty creature. If only that harridan were absent, I would say more.

Friske

Sweet sir, if she were absent, I would do more.

Prig

What a condition we are in. They will ravish him.

Friske

Are we not uncivil to leave Lucy? If you will go to her, I will come presently.

Striker

I am not to be taught civility by you. Go to her yourself, since you suggest it.

Trim

We are like to have very honest constant mistresses.

Prig

We are likely to get the clap.

Striker

I wonder at your impertinence.

Friske

My impertinence! You are a confident creature.

Striker

You are beneath my anger.

Mrs. Scroop

Ladies, ladies, let this go no farther.

Prig

Time to appear or he'll have them both else.

Trim

What, at war, ladies?

Prig

(to Friske) Madame, I see you can be gracious to the captain, though you are cruel to me.

Striker

What! Because I show a little outward civility. (to captain) But, captain, as we were saying—

Trim

You are most infinitely taken with the captain.

Striker

How dare you come here and stage a jealous scene? Begone.

Friske

(to Prig) Would you not have one well-bred?

(to captain) But, captain, you were saying something to me, even now.

Prig

Excellent! We must rout this captain or lose our whores.

Trim

Damn these young officers. All the whores run mad after them even though they don't have a penny or have the quaintest conception how to dress.

(Prig and Trim expostulate with Striker and Friske. They exit. Enter Lucy.)

Lucy

Sweet captain, I have no time to stay, nor dare I been seen alone with you. But this letter will tell you something. Farewell.

(Exit Lucy. Mrs. Scroop reads the letter with amazement. Sir Humphrey enters at another door with Sir Christopher and Tope.)

Sir Humphrey

(to Tope) And so, you have married Lady Cheatly?

Tope

(to Sir Humphrey) Ay, but mum's the word.

Sir Humphrey

Captain, your most humble servant.

Sir Christopher

(pouring beer or wine from a flagon on the table) Here's your health, captain.

Mrs. Scroop

You must excuse me, I never drink.

Tope

A captain and cannot drink? Can you whore?

Mrs. Scroop

Well enough for a beginner.

Sir Christopher

Not drink! A man is not fit for a captain that cannot drink. Shall I ask you a question?

Mrs. Scroop

Yes.

Sir Christopher

Can you fight?

Sir Humphrey

No bullying here, cousin.

Mrs. Scroop

You had best try, if you dare. What a question was that!

Sir Christopher

I have done. I have done.

(aside) If only Captain Hackum were here.

Mrs. Scroop

(angrily) It is not your best way to question it. I've killed men for less. And, sir, I don't like the way you're wearing your wig.

Sir Christopher

(terrified) He'll cut my throat.

(aloud) Sir, I beg your pardon.

Mrs. Scroop

(adjusting Sir Christopher's wig in a comical way) It becomes you better than way, don't you think?

Sir Christopher

Much, much better, captain.

Mrs. Scroop

Sing us a song.

Sir Christopher

A song, a song. Of course, a song.

(singing) I love somebody, I love nobody, Be she black, or be she brown, She's the best in all the town, So she keep her belly down, Down, down, down.

Mrs. Scroop

A very merry fellow. Give me your hand and be friends.

Sir Christopher

(visibly relieved) With all my heart.

Mrs. Scroop

Bring in the usurer. You shall see my new soldier exercised.

(Enter Scroop, between two soldiers.)

Scroop

Well, there's a law, sir.

Mrs. Scroop

Do you talk of law again? (striking him with the swagger stick)

Scroop

Hold, hold, hold, I say no more.

Mrs. Scroop

The next tide, he sails for Flanders.

Sir Christopher

Honest cousin Scroop, are you turned soldier? Shame, at your age, to play such tricks.

Tope

A very pretty soldier and stands lustily under a musket.

Scroop

(muttering) Well, I shall outlive this.

Mrs. Scroop

Order your arms. Did you ever see such a clumsy rogue? Take that to make you more skillful. (striking Scroop again)

(Scroop mutters.)

Mrs. Scroop

Poise your musket. Rascal, that's the wrong shoulder. (striking him again)

Scroop

I am so inept you had better discharge me.

Mrs. Scroop

I'll make you do it. Shoulder, I say. March.

Scroop

(trying to walk out) With all my heart.

Mrs. Scroop

Halt! Halt, you rogue, or I hang you for desertion.

Prig

Make him do double-time.

Scroop

Did you not bid me march?

Mrs. Scroop

I'll march you. Right into the mouth of a cannon before I have done.

Sir Humphrey

Admirable discipline, captain.

(Enter Valet, Captain Hackum, Sergeant Bluffe.)

Valet

Sir Christopher, take care. There are a dozen bailiffs surrounding the house. There is no possibility of escape.

Bluffe

It's true, there is no way out.

Sir Christopher

I can't go to jail.

Tope

Jail is a bad place. You will starve for good drink.

Hackum

There are too many for us to beat.

Sir Christopher

Captain, if you would but do us the favor of dressing us in red coats and owning us for your soldiers we may escape.

Tope

Excellent.

Mrs. Scroop

I cannot, in honor, pass you for my soldiers unless you be so. But if you will take a shilling and enlist, I may do it.

Sir Christopher

Gladly.

Hackum

With all my heart.

Mrs. Scroop

Here are shillings. Sergeant, procure some uniforms.

Sir Humphrey

You may command all my house.

Mrs. Scroop

Your humble servant.

Sir Christopher

Now, noble captain, we'll march under your command.

Mrs. Scroop

Come, you rogues. March, march, I say.

(They start to march out.)

Trim

(to Bluffe and Hackum) Oh, gentlemen, you are turned soldiers, I hear.

Sir Christopher

Rogue, we shall meet you.

Trim

I am glad to see you in this condition. Now one may safely keep company with you.

Mrs. Scroop

Who are you, sir? A soldier is in no condition to be laughed at by such an insect, a maggot, such as you.

Trim

A maggot! An insect! I am a knight, sir.

Mrs. Scroop

(cudgeling him) You are a rascal, sir.

(Mrs. Scroop leads out all the recruits. Enter Stanford.)

Stanford

Sir Humphrey, protect me. Hide me. I am fleeing from Sir Positive.

Prig

Oh, dear heart, I have met you. I have been seeking you all over town.

Stanford

What's this? I have to leave in great haste. Adieu.

Prig

Dear Jack, I have not so little honor as to leave you in such a condition

Stanford

What condition? I am not drunk, am I?

Prig

No, no.

(aside) Bluffe threatens to cut your throat about last night; and I am come to offer you the service of my sword and arm.

Stanford

What's this? He wouldn't dare. Do not trouble yourself or me.

Prig

It's no trouble.

(Enter Sir Positive.)

Stanford

I am in haste. I must run.

Sir Positive

Have I found you, Jack? Run? Why, will you pretend to running in my company? Why, I have run sixty miles in one day beside a lady's coach, and yet I was not winded all that time.

Stanford

I believe you.

Sir Humphrey

(to Prig and Trim) Let's tease Sir Positive.

Prig

(loud) But neither Trim nor Sir Positive understand mathematics like myself.

Sir Positive

Who's that talks of mathematics? I don't think you understand the principles on it. You are scarce come so far yet as the squaring of the circle. Why this is the only thing I value myself on in the whole world.

Sir Humphrey

Stand up to him in mathematics, to him.

Prig

Say you so? By the Lord Harry, sir Positive, I do understand mathematics better than you.

Sir Positive

Draw! I will justify with my sword that you understand nothing at all.

Sir Humphrey

Hold, Sir Positive.

Stanford

This affliction is beyond all example.

Tope.

Dear Sir Positive, I think you understand more than Solomon did.

Sir Humphrey

But, I am sure you know nothing of pastry.

Sir Positive

Pastry. I had thought I had kept that quality to myself. Sure the devil must help you. Why, damn it, devil take me if I would not be content never to eat pie but of my own making so long as I live. When I was but four years old I had so rich a fancy, and made such extraordinary dirt pies, that the most eminent chefs in all London would come to observe me and steal from me.

Trim

Steal!

Sir Positive

Steal? Well thought on. If I don't give you an account of thieving shall make you stare, cut my throat. It is the only thing I am proud of in the world.

Sir Humphrey

You are a man of universal knowledge, Sir Positive.

Sir Positive

(beaming with modesty) I, I? I understand but little.

Sir Humphrey

Now, Tope, to your post.

(Sir Humphrey and Tope stand on each side of Sir Positive.)

Tope

Navigation.

Sir Positive

(turning to Tope) Do you talk of navigation?

Sir Humphrey

Geography.

Sir Positive

(turning to Sir Humphrey) Who named geography? Do you talk of that science before me, when I invented it?

Tope

Astronomy.

Sir Positive

(volting face) I have studied it since childhood.

Sir Humphrey

Theology.

(before Sir Positive can speak) Metaphysics.

Tope

Surgery.

Sir Humphrey

Singing.

Tope

Logic.

Sir Humphrey

Legerdemain.

Tope

Palmistry.

Sir Positive

Hold, hold, hold. Navigation, Geography, Astronomy, Theology, Metaphysics, Magic. I'll speak to every one of them. If I don't understand everyone to perfection, if I don't fence, dance, ride, sing, speak Spanish, French, Dutch, Latin, Greek, Russian,

Gaelic, Hebrew, etc. Get me something to drink.

Stanford

Hell and damnation.

Sir Positive

Hold, hold, hold. I haven't told you half. If I don't do all these and fifty times more, I am the greatest owl, monkey, baboon, rascal, oaf, ignoramus, blockhead, buffoon, or what you will. Spit on me. Piss on me, I say, if I am not.

(They go out, Sir Positive running to keep up with them, talking as fast as he can. Enter by another door, Mrs. Scroop, who is pursued by Striker.)

Mrs. Scroop

What shall I do, these wenches will overrun me?

Striker

Dear Captain, I am transported by the assurance you gave me of having your love. You are the first to ever win my heart.

Mrs. Scroop

Seal the promise with a kiss.

Striker

Sweet creature, I can deny thee nothing. NOTHING!

Mrs. Scroop

A pity that troublesome creature Friske is always watching us.

Striker

Sir Humphrey has a large house. I know of a very secret place where I may show you more of my mind, and we may talk of—

Mrs. Scroop

Of?

Striker

Of...NOTHING!

Mrs. Scroop

That will give us time to do SOMETHING.

(They kiss as Friske enters.)

Striker

See. See. That envious bitch stalks us. Farewell. In an hour, in the gallery.

(Striker goes out, sticking her tongue out at Friske.)

Mrs. Scroop

Now that that malicious woman is gone, I can tell you how much I love you.

Friske

Me! What did you kiss her for then?

Mrs. Scroop

Because I wished to make a fool of her.

Friske

Did you so, dear Captain?

Mrs. Scroop

You are an angel compared to her. I would I were in bed with thee.

Friske

It is my wish, too, sweet Captain.

Mrs. Scroop

We are still watched. I will come to you in an hour in the long gallery. You shall find me a lion.

Friske

And I will be your lamb. Here comes Lucy. Farewell.

(Exit Friske. Enter Lucy. They bow coyly to each other.)

Lucy

Sweet Captain.

Mrs. Scroop

I hate to injure Sir Humphrey, but I am so taken with you that I must risk my honor. Will you meet me in the gallery in an hour?

Lucy

Sure there's witchcraft in you.

Mrs. Scroop

I hate to be ungrateful to Sir Humphrey. I have so many obligations to him.

Lucy

Never think in that; who shall tell him? We are watched. I must go.

(Exit Lucy, enter Sergeant.)

Mrs. Scroop

(aside) Why, I will tell him. But, I have a trick will make this whore his wife.

(aloud) Well, Sergeant? Has my husband capitulated?

Sergeant

Not yet. He bid me cut his throat rather than agree to a separate maintenance.

Mrs. Scroop

Old dotard! If he's not careful, I'll let you.

Sergeant

I told him he must, or sail for Flanders where he would surely die in action, if lucky, or at the Captain's hand, if not so lucky. I left him cursing.

Mrs. Scroop

'Tis a great question whether he prefers to die or part with the money.

Sergeant

If he yields not, I will take him, sister.

Mrs. Scroop

Come, where are my soldiers? I must lose no time.

(Sergeant goes out and brings in Scroop, Bluffe, Sir Christopher and Hackum) We are for Flanders, lads, and action.

Scroop

I am not for Flanders and action, but for mortgage actions.

Mrs. Scroop

Do you mutter?

Scroop

Hold, I will obey.

Sir Christopher

Come, Captain, have done with us, now you have owned us before the bailiffs.

Bluffe

Good, bully, Captain, you overacted your part before the bailiffs and laid on too hard, let me tell you that.

Hackum

You broke my head.

Mrs. Scroop

Pshaw! That was nothing. You should see me when I am angry.

Sir Christopher

No matter, let that pass. But, now, let us be in earnest and sup in Alsatia; we'll have fiddles and whores to entertain you and roar like dragons.

(singing) Be she black, be she brown, She's the best in all the town.

(to Scroop) How's the old fool? Does the soldier's life agree?

Mrs. Scroop

(menacingly) I don't like your voice.

(Sir Christopher quakes and is silent.)

Stand to arms!

Sir Christopher

What the devil!

Mrs. Scroop

Handle your arms! Damme! Am I to be obeyed? (cudgeling them)

Sir Christopher

Are you mad? Leave off fooling, Captain.

Mrs. Scroop

Handle your arms, all. (beating them)

Hackum

If you strike again, I'll draw.

Bluffe

I say the same.

Mrs. Scroop

Mutiny, eh? Musketeers, make ready.

(Enter several Redcoats with ready muskets.)

Sir Christopher

Make ready? What the devil do you mean?

Mrs. Scroop

(commanding the musketeers) Present.

Sir Christopher

Hold, hold, hold. I'll obey.

Bluffe

We'll obey.

Hackum

Hold.

Mrs. Scroop

No trifling with me. Shall such rascals as you think to be brave by being drunk and beating the watch?

Sir Christopher

Good Captain, we did not intend to be soldiers, only to escape the watch.

Mrs. Scroop

If I let you go, I would be four men short.

Sir Christopher

It was a joke.

Mrs. Scroop

I never joke.

Bluffe

Pox on your project.

Hackum

We had better fought the bailiffs.

Mrs. Scroop

You took the money. It is impossible I should be four men short.

Sir Christopher

Who the devil would have thought it? A pitiful little fellow; I could beat two on him.

Mrs. Scroop

(to the musketeers) Ground your arms. Next mutiny I'll hang you all.

Bluffe

You can't do that, you'll be four men short.

Mrs. Scroop

No, no. I am not short if I hang you. The company is complete even if you are dead. It's in the rules.

Hackum

We'll obey.

Mrs. Scroop

I thought you would. Come, lads, handle your arms. Pose your muskets.

(to Sir Christopher, tapping him playfully as he cringes) Wrong shoulder, sot.

Scroop

What will become of me? Heaven help me.

Mrs. Scroop

March. To the right. To the right. Now, rascal, you are to the left. What would you do?

Sir Christopher

What would you have?

Mrs. Scroop

Now, march them to their quarters and set a guard on them.

(Mrs. Scroop and the recruits all go out at one door. Enter Sir Humphrey at another. Sir Humphrey is in a pleasant mood. Enter Valet hurriedly.)

Valet

I bring you news that will stop you in your career of mirth.

Sir Humphrey

(easily) What do you mean? No more moralizing, I hope?

Valet

All your land in Essex is seized on by your creditors. After the settlement you made on Miss Lucy, you have nothing left.

Sir Humphrey

(alarmed) Is this true?

Valet

Too true.

Sir Humphrey

Well, well. A desperate ill must have a desperate cure.

(Enter Lucy. Exit Valet by another door.)

Sir Humphrey

I must confer with you about something that concerns your honor and our love.

Lucy

And I am to tell you something that concerns my honor and your want of love.

Sir Humphrey

What?

Lucy

Do you think I am to be treated like a kept woman?

Sir Humphrey

I have not treated you so.

Lucy

You must know, sir, I look upon myself to be, in a manner, your lady.

Sir Humphrey

(flabbergasted) Very well.

Lucy

And, do you imagine I will suffer such debauchery and wickedness in my house?

Sir Humphrey

How long has it been your house?

Lucy

Since you were pleased to make it so; and it is as much mine as if it had been in my family these five hundred years.

Sir Humphrey

To whose bounty do you owe it?

Lucy

To no bounty. I owe it to my bounty and my virtue.

Sir Humphrey

Most excellent.

Lucy

Shall I throw away the flower of all my youth on you for nothing? In short, I am to let you know this is my house and I will have no abominations committed here! I will not have your lewd sotting companions and, above all, I will not have whores brought into my house.

Sir Humphrey

I hope the sin you speak of is not so great—for your sake!

Lucy

Your sister and mother shall be welcome, provided they give me the respect which is due me. But, as for those ill-bred kept things, Striker and Friske, know that they must never come here again.

Sir Humphrey

Who is it that kept you?

Lucy

My exquisite beauty.

Sir Humphrey

Are you not a tailor's daughter?

Lucy

My present fortune makes me a lady in this town. And, I am sure I was born with the heart of a queen.

Sir Humphrey

(grabbing her by the wrist) Very well, madame, Since you are grown so pious and reformed, I will bring you to confer with a learned churchman to discuss a case of conscience. I will not allow you to continue to live in a state of mortal sin. Pray you come along with me.

(Sir Humphrey hauls her out somewhat roughly.)

Lucy

It seems I shall be your lady in good earnest.

(Exit Sir Humphrey and Lucy. Enter Mrs. Scroop with Mr. Scroop. Mrs. Scroop is dressed as a woman.)

Scroop

Perfidious jade. Why are you here?

Mrs. Scroop

(caressingly) My dear, look not so strangely. I am come to beg my brother to release you.

Scroop

My dearest wife. I am transported to receive you back. (aside) I think strangling her will be a very good death.

Mrs. Scroop

Can you forgive me for running away?

Scroop

I shall love thee as well as I ever did. (aside) Perhaps I might run her through and say she killed herself.

Mrs. Scroop

My brother now has prisoned me because I told him I would get a warrant for your release.

Scroop

Dear heart, I shall never forget this.

(aside) Let me see, a small knitting needle under her left arm when she's asleep will do the business rarely.

Mrs. Scroop

There's no way left but to seem to comply.

Scroop

Comply. I'll go to Flanders.

Mrs. Scroop

He told me he means to throw you off the boat and say you were lost at sea.

Scroop

The devil. I cannot swim.

Mrs. Scroop

I know, poor sweetheart. Therefore, pretend to sign. I don't want to lose you. It's nothing to your fortune. Only four thousand pounds.

Scroop

Nothing!

(aside) if I should smother her with a pillow and give out she died of apoplexy! That's the most secret way I have thought on yet.

Mrs. Scroop

He's so hotheaded he may deliberately drown you. He said something about keel hauling. What is that?

Scroop

Keel hauling is when you're dragged under the ship. It's terrible. He wouldn't dare.

Mrs. Scroop

He'd dare.

Scroop

Let him do it. Let him do it. Four thousand pounds. Let him do it, I say.

Mrs. Scroop

(aside) I see his life will be on my conscience.

(aloud) I'll give it back to you, dear one. Just sign it to appease him.

Scroop

Will you so? Here, kiss me. That's a dear wife.

(aside) I have it sure now. I'll give her opium in her drink and neither doctor nor surgeon can discover when they open her. It shall be so!

Mrs. Scroop

Trust me. I'll restore the deed. We are one flesh.

Scroop

Sweet lamb. I long to get you home safely. (aside) Well, she takes opium, that's certain, for while she lives, I shall walk in fear of her brother.

(Enter Sergeant.)

Sergeant

Your brother wants you, madame.

(Exit Mrs. Scroop.)

Sergeant

(leading Scroop out by another door) You go to your post, recruit.

(Sergeant and Scroop exit. Enter Lady Cheatly.)

Lady Cheatly

Where is Mr. Tope?

Servant

(entering) I'll find him for you.

(Enter Tope.)

Tope

Dearest Honora, I saw you from the window.

Lady Cheatly

Sweet Jack.

(Enter Steward.)

Steward

Have I tracked you here?

Lady Cheatly

Is this villain returned?

Steward

Yes, perfidious women. I am returned. Did you think to have me clapped under the hatches and carried to the Indies to be sold as a slave? Well, it didn't work. Come, madame. I will make you know your lord and master.

Lady Cheatly

What in the world are you talking about, poor man? You must be feverish or drunk.

Steward

Drunk. Know your duty, wife.

Tope

Your wife? Why, I fancy till yesterday you were her servant.

Steward

What fellow is this? I don't care to have such old sots about my wife.

Lady Cheatly

Definitely mad. Call a constable and take him to Bedlam.

Steward

Do not persist in your impudence.

Tope

You are very saucy to your lady.

Steward

Saucy to my wife? Peace, old fool.

Tope

Fool, eh? Old fool, eh?

Lady Cheatly

Impudent villain. Your wife?

Steward

Audacious woman, do you dare to deny it? Was I not married to you last night in your own chamber by a parson?

Lady Cheatly

What an impudent lie. Where did you dream this?

Steward

(stupefied) You deny it?

Lady Cheatly

(innocently) Most assuredly I'll deny it—and you shall never prove it. Marry you!

Steward

I'll ruin you.

Lady Cheatly

It's out of your power, fool.

Steward

I'll find that parson if he be in England.

Tope

But he's not.

Steward

Not in England? Have you sent him to France?

Tope

(pulling his hat over his face, in a quavering voice) Do you take this woman...ha, ha, ha. At your service, dear sir.

Steward

You! You were the parson?

Lady Cheatly

My most private chaplain. Could you think I would so far lose my breeding as to marry such a fellow as you are?

Steward

The marriage is good. I'll bring you to court to swear to it, sir.

Tope

If you do, ten to one, I'll foreswear it, sir.

Steward

You dare not.

Tope

By heaven, I do. Men foreswear themselves to get whores and make nothing on it. I shall foreswear myself to get such a widow. What man would not? She is mine. Now, begone.

Steward

I will have you my wife or be revenged. I am going to visit all those you have had business with this month and acquainted them with certain facts that will interest them mightily.

(Exit Steward.)

Tope

Shall I cut his throat?

Lady Cheatly

No. Stop his mouth, however, you must, or he'll invent a thousand lies about me; get him arrested for theft.

Tope

Fear not. I'll do as becomes a gentleman and have him hanged.

(Exit Tope. Enter Trim.)

Trim

Not all the clouds in the firmament can hide the sun, so nothing can obscure my Dorinda's glories or conceal the radiant luster of her conquering beams.

Lady Cheatly

I see to the quick-sighted Eugenius, nothing is obscured.

Trim

I am not a little afflicted that I have been constrained to bar myself so long from your lady's presence.

Lady Cheatly

(aside) It were pity to neglect this opportunity. Tope will be busy.

(aloud, languishing) Mr. Trim, your absence has been most afflicting.

(Enter Prig and Sir Positive.)

Sir Positive

Ah, there you are, divine Honora. Now you can hear the music I prepared for you yesterday.

Lady Cheatly

(to Trim) Heaven help us. I hate his music worse than the creaking of a barn door.

Trim

I'll get rid of him. (to Sir Positive) Sir, you are too familiar. Your apish gesticulations are not welcome to Lady Cheatly.

Sir Positive

This will not stir me. I know you are not in earnest.

Trim

You might easily have collected that I am a person who is superior to you in music as I am to you in dress; you should not be so impudent as to offer to compose music in my presence.

Sir Positive

What do I hear?

Lady Cheatly

Incomparable.

Trim

Your impudence has ruffled and disordered the wonted serenity of my temper or I should not tell you that I have more knowledge of divinity, astrology, mathematics, and geography than you will ever have the luck to acquire if you sedulously study these next twenty years.

Sir Positive

Have you the impudence to say you are a better divine, astrologer, mathematician, and geographer than I am?

Trim

Aye, and not only that, but a better lawyer, statesman, navigator, clock-maker, and architect. Take not of that.

Prig

And what will break your heart, I am a better pastry cook. There, again, Sir Positive.

Trim

In a word, I understand everything that is or is not—better than you do. Take that from me.

Sir Positive

Impudence. What will this age come to? I am amazed.

Trim

I would not have you pretend to things you do not understand. What do you think of that?

Sir Positive

(drawing) Dogs! Now you see how wisdom chastises ignorance.

Lady Cheatly

Dear Sir Positive, calm yourself.

Trim

Hold, dear rogue. I did but droll with thee. By the Lord Harry, I take you to be one of the pillars of the nation.

Sir Positive (mollified)

Oh, do you so?

Prig

I beg your pardon a thousand times. There never was a man of more prodigious understanding.

Sir Positive

I knew it was impossible you should be in earnest. But, do you hear, have a care of being positive. A man would think you would learn more modesty of me.

(Enter Mrs. Scroop dressed as a captain, with the Sergeant, Scroop, Bluffe, Hackum, and Sir Christopher.)

Mrs. Scroop

Come, Sergeant, get the barge ready.

Scroop

What shall I do? If I seal that deed and ever get her into my hands again, I'll have her life. But, four thousand pounds—

Mrs. Scroop

Come, soldiers, it is time to go.

Scroop

Hold, hold. There's no remedy. I will sign.

(Scroop signs and seals.)

Mrs. Scroop

You must release these gentlemen for the riot at your house. Sign.

Scroop

(signing) Very well. I release them.

Mrs. Scroop

(throwing off her disguise) And now, Mr. Scroop, your abused wife civilly thanks you for her liberty.

Scroop

She dies, that's flat.

Friske and Striker

A woman!

Mrs. Scroop

But, I wish myself a man for your sakes.

Sir Christopher

Cudgeled by a woman!

Hackum

Were ever brave men so dishonored?

Sir Christopher

I will break all her windows every night for a year.

Sergeant

No, you will not, you dogs. I am Captain Wildfire, and you are my recruits. You took a shilling.

Sir Christopher

Good Captain, release us. We'll love and honor her if you release us.

Bluffe

We shall form her bodyguard.

Hackum

On my honor.

Sergeant

I am acquainted with your honor—and know your worth. Well, I will release you, but if you cause my sister any harm, I will slit your noses.

Hackum

We shall love her like a queen.

(Enter Sir William.)

Sir William

What's this I see!

Bluffe

Bear up to him. Bow, wow.

Hackum

Do not flinch. Bow, wow.

Sir Christopher

Bow, wow.

Sir William

Impudent rascal.

Sir Christopher

Go strike your dogs and call them names. You have nothing to do with me; I am of age.

Sir William

Am I not your father?

Sir Christopher

Yes, and a tenant for life of my estate. Be sure you commit no waste.

Sir William

Let me come at him.

Bluffe

So long as you forebear all violence. But, if you strike, we will defend him.

Sir William

Rascals. Villains. Were you not educated like a gentleman? Did I not beget you?

Sir Christopher

You educated me like a country sot. As to whether you begot me or not, I think you should refer to my mother. Let us hope the old jade had better taste.

Sir William

You ungracious wretch.

Sir Christopher

Shall my cousin be the bravest knight in Christendom and I be your flap–doodle, your country bumpkin?

Sir William

To break with me, when I had just arranged a marriage with your cousin Emilia, Lady Cheatly's daughter!

Bluffe

He's a notorious liar. Don't believe him.

Hackum

It's a trick to get you into his power.

Sir Christopher

No, no, daddy, I understand your shams; but, to talk fairly, in all occurrences of this nature, which either may or may not be, according to the different accidents which intervene, from whence either good or bad in and of themselves such things occur: Now since all this is premised, let us proceed to the matter in hand. (giggling)

Sir William

(in a fury) Prodigious impudence. Dogs, villains. I'll to the Lord Chief Justice.

(Sir William stalks out.)

Bluffe

Admirably carried on.

Hackum

Bravely done.

Sir Christopher

I begin to banter pretty well, eh?

Bluffe

Rarely.

Sir Christopher

I have married already an heiress provided me by my friends.

Sir William

(returning) A whore, no doubt.

Sir Christopher

Not so, neither. Tell him, Bluffe.

Bluffe

She's a very great lady.

(guffawing) She's Captain Hackum's sister.

Sir Christopher

Have you betrayed me?

(with genuine pain) I took you to be my friends.

Hackum

Dear brother-in-law, I am eternally at your service.

Prig

My old mistress. Sir Christopher, be patient. You will have a son and heir of mine shortly. Breed him up well, give him a good education.

Sir William

Fare you well. I give you joy sir.

(starts to leave, but sees Friske and returns) Friske, here? I'll not suffer her to stay in such company.

Bluffe

Do you come back?

Sir William

To find someone, that's all. My business with you is done.

Hackum

Looking for the woman with the whips?

Sir William

Death, I shall be a byword.

Sir Positive

Let me ask you one civil question?

Sir Christopher

Who is the schoolmistress with the whips? I have a lad needs breeding up.

Sir William

You are all a parcel of whoresons.

Hackum

This virtuous gentleman taken with a dominatrix? His son's own whore.

Sir Positive

Do you talk of birching?

Hackum

He loves to mortify his flesh, the old saint.

Trim

(sadly) I am sorry a person of your gravity is exposed to so much ridicule.

Sir William

You are all rogues and strumpets. What do you walk in a company of owls for? Come, Friske.

Hackum

(jeering) It was better in the last age.

(Friske is dragged out by Sir William. Tope enters and goes directly to Lady Cheatly.)

Tope

So, it seems I have married a beggar. Do not argue. Your steward has convinced me.

Lady Cheatly

All that he said was true. I am worth little or nothing.

Tope

This sham was well carried on.

Lady Cheatly

If you will go on and maintain what I have done, I shall have a great estate yet, though of right it belongs to others.

Tope

Say you so? Right! 'Tis no matter of right, I'll show them the law. Ladies and gentlemen: please know that I am married to this great heiress and beautiful lady. I give you Mrs. Tope.

(Everyone applauds.)

Sir Positive

Well, I am out in this, though it be for the first time in my life. I thought to have married her myself.

Lady Cheatly

I know how disappointed you must be, Mr. Trim.

Trim

Disappointed, pshaw. It is time to confess that last night I resigned my person to your daughter, and made her my wife. I hesitated to tell you for fear it would break your heart, because I knew you had designs on me for yourself. I ask your blessing, mother.

Lady Cheatly

Mother! I'll order you.

(Emilia and Stanford who have been standing in the doorway come forward.)

Emilia

We ask your blessing, too.

Lady Cheatly

These sluts have snapped up all the game in sight.

(Enter Sir Humphrey with Lucy.)

Sir Humphrey

Call all my servants. Now, take notice of this. I am (indicating Lucy) married to this lady.

Tope

How, married, too?

Sir Positive

To his wench?

Sir Humphrey

You seem to wonder at my proceeding. I found myself involved on a sudden beyond redemption and, therefore, chose this expedient. This she pirate robbed me of what my extravagance had let free.

Tope

Good, good, ha, ha, good. Hey, brave matrimony! Oh, rare matrimony! Oh, gallant matrimony! Oh, delicate matrimony! Oh, heavenly matrimony!

Mrs. Scroop

I wish you joy.

Sir Humphrey

She is the greatest fortune I could have gotten.

Striker

It is an honor to our profession.

Mrs. Scroop

You fool. I bribed your steward to tell you your estate was in the hands of your creditors, in hopes you would be driven to this. Enjoy your whore—I mean your wife. Here is a letter which will acquainted you better with the prospects of getting your own children. (giving him a letter) She gave this to me in all secrecy not an hour hence.

Sir Humphrey

Hell and damnation.

Mrs. Scroop

I am revenged. Learn, all men, by this example not to scorn your mistress or to beat your wife.

CURTAIN

EPILOGUE

Sir Positive

Ladies and gentlemen, I am an ass, an idiot, a blockhead, if I don't understand dramatic poetry of all things in the world.

Great plays, like great wits, have a mixture of madness in them. (I found that out myself, for about three years ago, I was as mad as ever a man was—and 'twas not above twelve months since that my brains were settled again, into their present orderly state.) And let me tell you, ladies and gentlemen, if any dramatic poem exists that has ever been, that has such characters, such images, such humor, such intrigues, such romance, such surprises—then I am no judge! No, I understand nothing in the world.

Notwithstanding it may be damned by the malice of this age, this play shall act with any play of Jonson's, Dryden's, Moliere's, Plautus', Terence's, Menander's Aristophanes—hold, hold—I'll have Shakespeare in, too.

I had like to have forgot that.

I have thought on it and considered it and made it my chief study since childhood. This is the funniest play that ever was made. And, between you and me, it's because I dictated every word of it to the author.

Talk no more of it. Give us your applause.

ABOUT THE AUTHOR

Frank J. Morlock has written and translated many plays since retiring from the legal profession in 1992. His translations have also appeared on Project Gutenberg, the Alexandre Dumas Père web page, Literature in the Age of Napoléon, Infinite Artistries.com, and Munsey's (formerly Blackmask). In 2006 he received an award from the North American Jules Verne Society for his translations of Verne's plays. He lives and works in México.

www.ingramcontent.com/pod-product-compliance
Lightning Source LLC
LaVergne TN
LVHW041614070426
835507LV00008B/234